MARGARET POWELL
IN AMERICA

Also by Margaret Powell

BELOW STAIRS

CLIMBING THE STAIRS

TREASURE ABOVE STAIRS

MARGARET POWELL'S COOKERY BOOK

MARGARET POWELL'S LONDON SEASON

SWEET MAKING FOR CHILDREN

MY MOTHER AND I

MARGARET POWELL

Margaret Powell
in America

London
MICHAEL JOSEPH

First published in Great Britain in 1973
by Michael Joseph Ltd
52 Bedford Square, London W.C.1

© 1973 by Margaret Powell

ISBN 0 7181 1172 9

Printed in Great Britain by
Richard Clay (The Chaucer Press) Ltd
Bungay, Suffolk

Contents

Introduction

When I told my relations and friends that I was going to America, their first comment was, 'You never are!' Which, in a way, was the right response, as I, too, never really believed in the possibility.

There was I, in London, having lunch with two young men: Toby, my agent, and Edmund my publisher, neither of whom did I know at all well; I'm not sure that I do now, come to that.

I must admit that Toby can order food and wine better than almost anybody I know. But this perfection was ruined by hearing him say, 'You don't mind if Edmund and I talk business?'

Well, of course I minded, unless it was my business, which it wasn't. I more than minded; I was inwardly seething with rage. Where was the point of being taken out by two young men, if no part of their conversation was being devoted to me?

Still, there are always compensations. While Toby and Edmund were engrossed in their business, I managed to drink more than my fair share of the wine and had just started on the delicious beef fillet when I heard Toby say, 'How do you feel about this American trip, Margaret?'

I looked around for this other Margaret: I knew it wasn't me. Then Toby actually turned and looked at me. 'Well, come on! What do you think? Would you like to go to America?'

'Oh, of course, my love,' I dreamily answered. But then I always say yes to any suggestion of Toby's although I seldom intend to do anything about it, if it conflicts with what I want to do.

'Of course,' Toby added, 'you will have to read a few books about America before you go. Can you do that?'

'Most certainly, love,' I murmured somewhat hazily, pouring myself yet another glass of wine. 'I do know how to read, so why not?'

Why not, indeed? Why not Timbuktu, the Fiji Isles and other exotic places? All stations west, I thought; I'll go to them all in my dreams.

'I'll come with you for the first three weeks, and then Michael can take over.' Michael also belongs to the clan. 'Right, that's all settled, then. Edmund and I have been making the arrangements.'

I was not really taking in a word of all this, being far more concerned with the problem of what liqueur to have with my coffee. Not that Toby had as yet offered me one, but he was going to—or else.

Suddenly I realized they were actually talking about me.

I floated home on a cloud, but very soon sense asserted itself. Of course Toby had never mentioned my going to America; or had he? If not, what did he say? Yes, on second thoughts, I'm sure he said that I was to write a book on my impressions.

I told Albert about this. What an angel that man is! Does he say to me, 'Not on your life you're not going. Only over my dead body do you go all those miles without me'? He does not; he says, 'Well, my love, that will be marvellous for you, but for heaven's sake take care of yourself. I want you back as good as you went. Don't let those young men work you too hard.'

I told my mother the news. Does she say, 'How marvellous'? She does not. 'What about Albert? What's he going to do while you are gallivanting all over America? Who will look after him? He's not getting younger you know. I would never have left your dad for six weeks.'

'Don't make me laugh! Chance would have been a fine thing,' and I argue with her—which she loves. 'What you really mean is that you never had the opportunity to go gallivanting all over America, so why should your daughter? Anyway,' I went on, 'Albert might get younger having a rest from me. He can reserve all his energy.'

Toby was soon on the phone, loftily informing me that *he* had

changed the date, and *he* would be making *new* arrangements. As I had never believed in the existence of the old ones, all this information was as nothing to me, just words.

But, pretending to everybody that I really was going, I listened to all the know-alls and their views of America.

Some said, '*If* you go, you'll hate it over there. Nobody's got any time for you; the cost of living is prohibitive, and you daren't walk in the street alone at any time of the day. As for the blacks, they are everywhere.'

Then I heard, '*If* you do go, you will find it's a wonderful country; no inhibitions, you can do anything you like when you like.' I thought that was a bit too late for me.

In any case, I considered that all this discussion was nothing but a waste of breath. The plan would never come to anything; I couldn't possibly be going to America.

Nevertheless, when the time drew near, I packed all my clothes; even although Albert kept on, 'What are you packing for if you're not leaving England?'

'Why?' was my thought, too. But still, one morning I found myself in a car with my sister and Albert on the way to Heathrow Airport.

1: Departure

There is something about an airport that fills me with a sense of my own inadequacy. I feel an anachronism, obviously out of my time in this computer age. I feel it is a place for machines only. Everywhere are displayed instructions that are supposed to convey information telling travellers when to depart and where from, but I can never find a sign that applies to my journey. Sometimes I have felt that I am in a kind of fourth dimension, invisible to those around me. Yet other people seem to manage the system. They show no anxiety; they get to the right gate at the right time. What I really need is a personal walkie-talkie, so that I can receive, for me only, a constant flow of plain and simple instructions that guide me down those endless corridors and on to the plane.

So when I arrived at Heathrow to start on my grand tour of America, I wasn't in the least surprised to find that Toby was nowhere to be seen; I had never really expected to see him, nor, indeed, had even been convinced that I would ever get to merica. Why should I have thought that I would? Toby I had own only a few weeks; I had no plane ticket; even the name of travel agency was a mystery to me. Nevertheless, I decided it a while, just in case a miracle occurred. It has been to. After about fifteen minutes I noticed that none of the there seemed to be departing. Had all the pilots gone on

king enquiries I discovered that I was in the wrong his was for arrivals only. Well, it can happen to anybody. I went up to a man who looked as though the milk of human kindness had not yet turned permanently sour, and asked the way to the departure building. What a charming man he was! He commiserated with me on the lack of information and said that only after dozens of plane trips had he managed to be in the right place at the right time. He gave me his card; people are always giving me their cards. Why haven't *I* got a card to hand over? I must do something about it if only so that he, or she, will remember me.

I was given detailed instructions. 'You go down the steps, turn to the left, follow the crowd and you can't miss it.' He didn't know me. I could have just as easily have followed the crowd into the car-park. However, I managed to find the right place.

Just imagine my relief when I was instantly recognized by the travel agent—for which heaven be praised—though still no sign of Toby. When he eventually did show up I was certain that it was to say he would not be coming, so casually was he dressed.

How shall I describe Toby? Well, he's tall and very slim—he manages to keep that way by not eating enough to keep a sparrow alive. He always appears to have been poured into whatever he is wearing. The only concession that he had made to this momentous occasion was to have his hair cut—a considerable improvement, I must admit, as on occasions he does resemble a wild man from Borneo. Apart from that, he was wearing a nondescript pair of jeans; an open-necked shirt; no tie; a far from smart jacket; and what appeared to be running shoes, rubber-soled canvas ones: the right attire for a stroll down the King's Road, maybe, but not for a journey of three thousand miles. That was my opinion anyway. Needless to say, I kept it to myself. The fact that he was there was enough.

To my astonishment and secret gratification, we were taken as though we were V.I.P.s to the Monarch Lounge, and served with drinks, too. At last I felt as though I might really be a traveller to America, though I couldn't understand why we had all this luxury. We were not travelling first-class. Nevertheless, I sure was happy to be downing a few drinks. It took my mind off the thought of flying over all that water.

I knew that I would be nervous at the take-off, but I naturally expected that Toby, my escort, would endeavour to allay my fears. What a hope! No sooner had we sat down than he proceeded to surround himself with books and papers, thus indicating to me that conversation would not be available on the voyage. He was starting as he meant to go on.

Although the plane had not yet moved, I was already feeling as though 'going over the top' was imminent. A quick look around at some of the passengers disclosed nobody who appeared apprehensive. It is a mistake to talk to somebody who has no nerves. You are better off if you can find a passenger even more alarmed than you are. This gives you a feeling of one-upmanship.

There was a man a few seats back who was wearing a deerstalker hat—you know, one of those hats with a peak back and front. Why is it made like that, I wonder. Is it so that a deer doesn't know whether you are coming or going? And why was the man wearing such a hat on a plane? Added to which he was so hirsute that, if he got down on his knees, a deer wouldn't have known him from the undergrowth. A few seats ahead were two nuns, dressed in the traditional voluminous black robes and hoods. From the manner in which they were fingering their beads I imagined that they were praying. Probably their prayers included all of the passengers, too. I was vaguely comforted at seeing representatives of the higher life aboard the plane. I felt that no harm could possibly happen to those two ladies who had obviously led a blameless life—either by chance or inclination—and had, perhaps, done actual good. So, if they had a safe journey, it would be safe for me too.

I saw the pilots come on board. One of them was young and handsome, but I preferred the older man. He looked the type who would have left behind a wife and family, and so naturally he would want to get back home safely just as much as I did.

A very pretty young lady was now pointing out the position of the emergency doors, unnecessary information as far as I was concerned; they were the first things that I located as soon as I got on the plane. Now she was showing us how to use the oxygen masks if we should need more air. I could sense that I was not going to need any extra breath to talk to my companion. He was as unconcerned about all these instructions for our safety as though he were on a bus ride to Fulham. I was so tense as the plane approached the runway that I was almost rigid with fright.

Did Toby notice? Not on your life! Far from being gifted with extra-sensory perception he appeared to be lacking in even ordinary perception.

As we taxied along, my past life floated before me like a mirage—well, those parts of it that were worth remembering.

The plane went faster and faster. I was speechless from fright and Toby was likewise from indifference. 'O death, where is thy sting?' I was murmuring to myself. 'We have overshot the runway,' when suddenly, we were in the air.

'We are actually flying,' I said to Toby, 'we're up.' I might as well have saved my breath. He just looked at me with a pained expression, as though he just couldn't understand why I should mention such an obvious fact.

Once we were airborne I became resigned to my fate. There was nothing that I could do now. In any case, food was being brought around. That always has the effect, if only temporarily, of taking my mind off my troubles. The meal was, to me at any rate, surprisingly good. We had smoked Scotch salmon; sauté of veal in Madeira sauce with mushrooms and olives; and for a sweet, meringues with real cream. We finished with coffee. Everybody consumed the food with great rapidity. Why are people so hungry on a plane. It must be nerves. For my part, I act on the saying that 'the condemned ate a hearty meal'. If there is a possibility that I may end up in a place where the food is nothing but nectar and ambrosia, it's as well to have a good solid meal before I depart. Drinks were brought round and were much appreciated by me, I can assure you. After two large brandies I began to feel as though life might still have something in store for me.

I endeavoured to get Toby into conversation, although I could sense that he had no desire to talk. I considered that it was his duty to tell me things about America. After all, I wouldn't have been on this hazardous assignment if it hadn't been for him. But it was a dead loss to hope for entertainment from Toby. In him the age of chivalry was dead, defunct and decomposed. He even moved back to an empty seat, on the excuse that he was tired and needed to sleep. But I was lucky. Seeing me on my own, the stewardess stopped to have a word. She must have recognized me, a great excitement for me now. Then I was invited on to the flight-deck and really felt a 'somebody'. The captain told me that his wife was one of my 'fans'. He alarmed me by saying that we were flying at 39,000 feet, though I couldn't really visualize such a height. But he then reassured me by saying, 'You know, B.O.A.C. may not be the highest-paid pilots, but they have the best pension scheme.' Here a voice interrupted, 'Yes, but we seldom live long enough to enjoy it.'

I completely lost all my fear of flying while sitting in the flight-deck surrounded by four men—I am never nervous of them. I really thought that I 'had it made' at last; there sure are fringe-benefits to becoming a familiar face—or is it voice?

For a change, instead of giving autographs, I collected four. The captain assured me that the reason that more females than males are invited on the flight-deck is not that the crew are sex-maniacs. 'The ladies don't ask awkward questions about the mechanics of flying. The men always want to know what this knob does or what that gadget is used for. Half the time I don't know myself what they are.' You can imagine that this remark did nothing to bolster my confidence that I would arrive at Boston. However, he couldn't have meant it seriously.

By the time that I returned to my seat, my ego was functioning in top form, and even more so when a first-class passenger came along to enquire why I was so privileged. I know it was nothing but vanity, but it did seem grand to be singled out from all those passengers. To board the plane an unknown Margaret Powell and suddenly to be recognized as a personality! To have people shake my hand and say how much they liked my books and seeing me on television! Well, I loved them all for being so nice and friendly.

I thought that even Toby would be impressed by this sudden fame of mine, that he might care to bask in my reflected glory. But not so. He took no notice. Well, one can't have everything! However, much to my glee, I got my revenge for this indifference. Toby had just returned to his seat next to me when a voice came over the loud-speaker, 'Congratulations on their golden wedding to Mr and Mrs—I'll call them Brown—sitting in seat Nos. 32A and B.' That was where Toby and I were sitting. Immediately there were roars of merriment from those passengers who could see us. I thought it was very funny but I don't think that Toby was delighted at being in the limelight.

The lady whose golden wedding it really was came to talk to me. It was pleasant to hear that both she and her husband liked my books. To celebrate their golden wedding their children were paying for them to have this trip to America. She loved flying and had never at any time felt nervous.

Why do I dislike flying? Perhaps a secret phobia remaining from the days of two boy-friends—at different times, of course—who both had 'hobbies'. The first one spent hours of his free time, time that should have been devoted to me, making model planes with balsa wood and glue. When they were finished there was nothing that you could do with them. You couldn't even fly them with an elastic band. He had these objects hanging down from the ceiling in his bedroom: nothing but dust-harbourers was my private opinion. He expected me to enthuse over this motley collection as though the hours he had spent on them would eventually benefit humanity. It wasn't even as though I could admire them in his bedroom in comfort. His mum, with her eagle eyes, was always hovering around the door.

Another young man not only made model planes; he actually flew them, too. Sunday after Sunday I was taken to Hampstead Heath, or Richmond, or some other place equally removed from civilization, while this Leonard, in company with other men equally besotted, set off the plane of the moment. There may be females who can feel exhilarated standing around in the cold wind and rain, steadily feeling their hair getting lank and faces more red, but I was not one of them. Yet these men—and some of them had long passed the age of consent—these enthusiasts were transfixed with joy if their particular plane stayed in the air for two minutes. Now I look back on it I must have been crazy. But such was the shortage of eligible males—or even ineligible ones—that, unless you had outstanding physical attributes to attract a male, you had to use other methods. Mine was to praise lavishly whatever footling hobby they were keen on. I hypocritically made it my hobby too, for as long as I thought there was a chance of a permanent relationship. Mind you, one couldn't afford to wait long. If a young man hadn't mentioned marriage within three months I looked for a more likely prospect.

I certainly expected that the journey cooped up in a plane would be somewhat tedious, but the time seemed to pass very quickly. I actually was brave enough to look out of the window as we approached Boston. I felt very excited but, unfortunately, with such a phlegmatic companion I had to suppress my feelings, as indeed I had to do throughout the entire trip.

2: Boston

However, I must admit that Toby was invaluable at the airport. He knew just where and how to get the luggage, how to get a taxi. To me it was marvellous to see Toby coping with all this as though to the manner born. But travelling is more than just being an expert at getting from one place to another. Travelling is absorbing the sights, sounds, even smells, the very essence of a new experience. This I was doing on the journey from the airport to the city of Boston. I was so excited at the thought of all I would be seeing and doing in America. I wanted to shout and sing. I needed a companion who, like me, had no real knowledge of this country.

I had come here last year with David Frost. But as the whole show was done on the plane going over I saw nothing of New York. I stayed just one night in Manhattan and never left the hotel. Now I was to be here nearly six weeks. Just think of my incredible good fortune! I tried to convey all this to Toby but it was hopeless to try to kindle any enthusiasm; he just grunted and went on reading business papers.

I cannot pretend that, in spite of my ignorance of the country, I had no preconceived opinions. Of course I had. With the spate of news about America that is written in newspapers and magazines and heard on the radio and television, I had my own idea of the country. It would be vast and noisy, one mass of huge cars, elevated railways and an underground system like an inferno. People couldn't breathe in the polluted atmosphere and those that did manage to live were in constant fear of sudden death by violence. Everybody was rushing madly from place to place with no time to talk to strangers, and all taxi-drivers and shop-assistants were rude. The architecture would be hideous, littered with neon signs, and culture was non-existent.

Against that would be palatial houses exuding the smell of money; every technological device one could think of servicing industry; and those out-of-this-world glossy kitchens displayed in our magazines.

So on this, my first glimpse, I looked at everything, determined to take it all in.

When we actually reached Boston it didn't at first sight present a clean and sparkling face. In the side-streets, and even some of the main roads, battered old dustbins littered the pavements—or sidewalks as they are called there. The contents were spilling all over the place and the gutters were full of rubbish. Afterwards I found out that the garbage-collectors and street-cleaners were on strike, but it was a bit of a shock to see this reality.

I liked the look of our hotel in Boston, The Lenox. It was not one of those very new and ornate places with entrances that put one in mind of a baronial hall. It still retained an old colonial style, with lovely brass chandeliers, real logs burning in the fireplace. And, most important, the staff seemed friendly. I remarked on this latter fact to Toby who attached no importance to it. I was finding out that he was impervious to outside influences.

Our first evening there we ate in an oyster-bar, packed like sardines with about a foot of bar-counter to each person; not exactly the meal of my dreams. I had visualized Boston as an old city, still living in the past, with quiet, elegant restaurants, candle-lit tables and deferential waiters. They have got these—well, perhaps not the deferential waiters. In this land of equality where Jack's as good as his master—if not better—everybody that waits on you, even to just serving you with a drink at the bar, expects a tip. Nevertheless, in spite of the crush, the food was very good. Here again Toby came into his own because he knows about food. Well, I know about English food. But all I know about American is hamburgers, doughnuts and waffles—not exactly a wide variety, or suitable for a dinner. Toby picked up the menu and nonchalantly went through the items. I ought, I know, to have appreciated his knowledge, but I didn't. I was already somewhat irritated at his I-have-seen-it-all-before air. If I hadn't been afraid of looking silly I'd have picked my own items, but I didn't want to risk starting off with what might have turned out to be a sauce.

Toby chose clam chowder for us to start with. It's a sort of fish soup, very well-flavoured. The next course on the menu was cherrystones. I hadn't a clue what they were; they might even have been a sweet. They turned out to be very small oysters, served with a horse-radish sauce so hot and pungent that I nearly went through the roof after swallowing the first mouthful. Toby warned me of the strength of the sauce too late, as he warned me too late of many other things.

Back in our hotel we decided to have a drink in what the management termed 'The Old English Pub, a charming replica of an old country pub'. The waiters were attired in a sort of loose white blouse, red waistcoat and breeches, and tight white leggings to the knees. What particular period of British history this gear was meant to represent was a mystery to me. Was it ever a period of British history? Perhaps the old coaching inns. Maybe the barmen were redolent of 'ye olde worlde', but not much else was. The seats were upholstered in some kind of plastic material, and, to add to the incongruity, a television set was over the bar and a long row of people sitting on stools were gazing at it without saying a word. Where was the atmosphere of an old English pub! In retrospect it was just like any American bar apart from the different décor. It's people that make a pub—those who own it, those who serve and their customers.

I just couldn't imagine an American barman waiting on the customers with the same kind of service that one gets in a real old English pub—not that there are so many of them left now. Where was the conversation? The 'Good evening! Lovely weather for the time of the year.' Here the barman came to our table, stood there without saying a word, took our order, brought it to us and walked off. He would be about as much at home in a country pub as I would be in an igloo.

One of the customers in the bar assured me that the television was used only on special occasions, such as the baseball game that they were viewing. Now that's a game which makes ordinary sane Americans who watch become metamorphosed into jumping jacks, judging by the way they act. Admittedly all I know about the game is that it appears to be somewhat like the rounders that we played at school—but less exciting. I watched for half an hour and nothing at all happened. There was this man wearing an oversized glove on one hand and throwing a ball to a man who held a kind of bat; he never did hit the ball once. He must have been meant to, surely. How Americans can say that our cricket is a slow game beats me. Before I left for America I met an American at a party who derided, though in the nicest possible way, our game of cricket. 'It's the ideal game to watch for a businessman like me.' 'Why so?' I said. 'Well, I can make a long-distance telephone call and know that when I look at the screen again I shall have missed nothing.'

Although my bedroom was so high up that the noise of the traffic was very faint, and my bed was the last word in comfort and large enough for two, I woke up at the crack of dawn. Determined not to waste a minute of time in idly lying about, I got dressed and sat at the window watching the people and cars. Surprisingly, even at that early hour there seemed to be a lot of both.

I noticed across the road an old English institution, a Muffin House. I decided that Toby and I would have our breakfast in this establishment. I waited until eight o'clock before telephoning through to his room because he certainly didn't appear to be the type that would gallop out of bed to greet the dawn chorus—or whatever was the equivalent in Boston. As there was no answer to my ring I thought that maybe he was already up and about. I searched the hotel downstairs but no sign of Toby. So I rang his room again. Still silence. So in disgust I went over to the Muffin House on my own, as it was now nearly nine o'clock. It took me some days to realize that I would seldom, if ever, breakfast with Toby, and that he had a rooted dislike to seeing a face that he knew sitting opposite him so early in the morning. Could be that's why he isn't married; can't bear the thought of breakfast for two. Nevertheless, although alone, I enjoyed my breakfast, including the muffins, of course. These were served in so many ways that the original old English muffin seemed lost. The place was full and the service good, though I would have liked a smile from my waitress. Still, as the shop opened at seven o'clock she had already been on her feet two hours.

I had my muffins served plain, but whether American muffins are different from English ones, or whether I am too old to appreciate them I don't know. Certain it was that they seemed to bear no resemblance to those the muffin man came around with on a Sunday afternoon. He would ring his bell along our street and Mum would send me out to buy a dozen. Cut in half and toasted, even although spread only with margarine, they were delicious.

While I was in this American Muffin Shop I was interested to see a very poverty-stricken old woman come in with a large paper bag and collect all the half-eaten muffins from the tables. None of the waitresses took any notice or attempted to turn her out, and I saw some of the customers giving her their whole muffins. I couldn't imagine an old lady going round a Joe Lyons collecting left-overs!

I suddenly realized that I had left only a one-cent tip in the Muffin House, so I decided not to venture in there again. It's this American money that confuses me. A five-cent piece is larger than a dime, yet that is worth ten cents.

On returning to the hotel, still feeling somewhat aggrieved that my first breakfast in America had to be on my own, I discovered Toby in the reception hall. From the look on his face you would have imagined that he was the injured party.

'Where on earth have you been?' he furiously asked. 'I have been ringing your room for the last hour. You shouldn't go out without telling me.'

I was still too nervous of him to answer as I would have liked to—that if he had been awake at a decent hour he would have got me; and as for telling him what I was doing—well, I certainly wasn't going to wait half the morning to do just that.

But Toby was still laying down the law. 'I've booked you on a Gray Line Tour and it leaves this hotel in five minutes. So if you have anything to do, be quick.'

By this time my normal equanimity was beginning to slip a bit, so I enquired in what to me sounded like a voice full of rage—only he didn't seem to notice it—'What about you then? Aren't you coming?'

But no, he wasn't coming. I'd do better on my own, and anyway he had things to do of vital importance to our stay in America.

I discovered eventually that this was to be the pattern of our days—me always doing Gray Line trips on my own. Toby arranged what I was to do, but I could never have a say in arranging anything for him—and certainly not coach trips. Why, he might even have to talk to ordinary people!

The tour that he had booked me on included a mile and a half of history about the American War of Independence. During the course of my stay in America I found that there was always a certain amount of hazard attached to going on one of these bus tours, starting with the driver, who is also the guide. He can be a driver who just gives out information and keeps quiet in between; or he can be, and often is, a driver who keeps up a non-stop flow of facetious humour. After an hour of this I was ready to scream, but to be honest, most of the passengers seemed to enjoy it. Then of course there is the hazard as to who sits next to you for two to three hours. I used to try to be one of the last to get into the bus; then if there were any lone males I sat down next to them. I found, by trial and error, that this worked very well, for either they never spoke a word to me, or were interested only in me. This failed on one occasion, but of that I shall write later.

Unfortunately, on this tour of the Freedom Trail there was only a seat next to a woman so fat that she occupied nearly three parts of the seat. Far from trying to disguise her size, she seemed to want to display it by wearing red trousers which bulged out her thighs, and a canary yellow blouse cut so low that very little was left to the imagination. Within five minutes she had informed me, in a voice as strident as a cockatoo's, that she came from New York; that she was in Boston visiting her daughter; that her grandchildren were the prettiest things; and that she suffered from blood pressure. Never had I heard a woman talk so fast. (Later on I discovered that a lot of Americans seem to speak very quickly. Perhaps it's that gum-chewing which keeps their jaws very pliable.) I did not enquire whether she suffered from high or low blood pressure, knowing full well that any sympathetic enquiry about people's ailments, real or imagined, will start them on a recital that goes on into infinity. As soon as she found that I was English the full flood of her oratory really engulfed me. 'Well now, isn't that something! I was over there myself last year; it sure is a quaint place.'

I murmured something to the effect that I had never realized it was quaint, that in fact I rather liked it.

'Sure, sure, but it's so old-fashioned, so behind the times. We stayed in several towns and never once did we find any central heating or air-conditioning. The coffee was goddamn awful and as for the food! On top of that it rained all the time and you couldn't get a drink in a bar after eleven o'clock.'

I was to hear all this many times before I left America. I came to believe that some Americans liked to boast about what they considered the primitive conditions to be found in England, the hardship they had endured. It made them feel superior and well-travelled.

Before I could think of what to say in praise of England the bus started on the Freedom Trail. The 'Freedom' is getting free from British dominance in the War of Independence. It certainly was strange to hear all about this from the American point of view and also somewhat disconcerting to hear a man in the next seat say, 'Best thing that ever happened to this country, when we got rid of the bloody British.' Still, as I'm not chauvinistic I wasn't seized with a patriotic fervour to assault him. In fact I very much enjoyed this mile and a half of history, from Boston Common where the soldiers were trained—and witches hanged— past the State House with its golden dome on to what is known as the Boston Massacre Site. Here a British guard fired into a jeering crowd, killing five people. With human life held so cheap, as it seems to be now, it seems strange to read that the death of five people was a 'massacre'.

Our driver-guide was very knowledgeable about this particular bit of American history, probably because he had to relate it day after day. I had read in our history books of the Battle of Bunker Hill, but I wouldn't have known it was the same battle from the way our guide was relating it. My sixth-form teacher was a great believer in the glorious British Empire. Maybe because she was about sixty and unmarried, she had little else to be enthusiastic about. She told us how King George III had been forced by his own Parliament to give America independence, and how ungrateful the Americans were in throwing us out of the country and refusing to be a part of our empire. So emotionally did Miss Green, our teacher, tell us about the Battle of Bunker Hill and how bravely the British fought against overwhelming enemy forces, that the climax came as a bit of a shock, when she had to tell us that the British were defeated. I know that I thought, 'How could we be defeated if we were the bravest and best?'

There are two hundred and ninety-four steps to the top of the Bunker Hill Monument and you have to pay ten cents to climb them. Some of the passengers were energetic enough to do this but I wasn't one of them; I had come out for pleasure, not punishment.

Somebody must have told the driver that there was an English person on the bus because over the loud-speaker he said that he hoped he wasn't offending anybody by his adverse comments on the British; it was all dead and gone now. It certainly didn't worry me, though I must admit that it did seem strange to realize that this Freedom Trail was freedom from us. I thought that we took pride in bringing freedom.

I wanted to see the actual place of the Boston Tea Party, where they threw all our tea in the river because they refused to pay the tax. Though from what I have read, tea wasn't noticeably cheaper from any other source. My seat-mate—'call me Effie'—wanted to see the oldest house in Boston; it is exactly the same today as it was when it was built in 1677. Here lived Paul Revere, renowned for his midnight ride to Lexington to warn the people that the British were coming. By this time Effie had worked herself up into a fever of patriotism for this potted version of 'How we threw out the British', though I very much doubt that in the normal way she opened a book of any kind. By the time that we reached the Granary Burying Ground, where are buried three men who signed the Declaration of Independence—John Hancock, Robert Paine and Samuel Adams—I was somewhat alarmed in case Effie knelt down to kiss the ground where they were interred. I wondered how she would manage to get on her feet again. As for me, I felt the sole representative of a nation of tyrants, the upholder of the monarchical principle and death to democracy. I made haste to assure Effie that none of my ancestors had fought in the War of Independence.

When I returned to the Lenox from this Gray Line Tour I discovered that Toby had decided that we should visit the opera, never mind about whether I wanted to do so—and I certainly didn't. I told him I had no ear for music and considered it ludicrous in the extreme for people to burst into song when they wished to communicate with each other. He said that it would be an experience for me, and that I couldn't expect to have one long round of pleasure. What pleasure? To me it seemed sheer waste of money on something that I knew in advance I would dislike, something, in fact, that could be positively harmful to me, inasmuch as, seeing hundreds of people enjoying an experience that meant nothing to me, I could very easily acquire an inferiority complex. Furthermore, as I pointed out, we would be depriving a rabid opera-lover of a seat. All this made no difference, because Toby, of course, adored opera.

The Boston Opera House is nothing like Covent Garden. It's a vast place, and I took a certain malicious pleasure at seeing Toby's dismayed expression when he realized we were so far away from the stage. It was like looking at it from the wrong end of a telescope. I knew that I would see only vague figures and probably hear little, but that caused me no grief. I never can understand a word even if it's rendered in English.

The opera was *Fidelio*, sung in German—most decidedly not an opera calculated to lighten one's burden of gloom, but a dark vengeful tale of violence and dungeons, with every song like a dirge.

Toby was irritated at the audience clapping at the end of each aria—or whatever they call that vocal eruption. He said that it wasn't the done thing; that it broke the thread of the plot. I couldn't see that it mattered at all. There was enough gloom on the stage without its extending into the audience—it had already spread to me.

I welcomed the interval, and as our admission ticket included a free glass of champagne we adjourned to collect it. Already the room was filling up with earnest devotees, all determined that the opera was splendid and the singers superb.

Fortunately for me, Toby, already incensed to find the stage so far away and the *hoi polloi* expressing their enthusiasm between the acts, now discovered that the so-called champagne tasted like over-ripe apples. So grabbing my arm and muttering, Toby left at once and we retired to Ye Olde English Pub, where, in spite of the absence of English I immediately began to enjoy myself.

We had an invitation to meet a very charming couple for lunch at the Ritz-Carlton. They were picking us up at ten o'clock for a drive around Boston and a visit to the Isabella Stewart Garden Museum. The thought of having to face life at ten o'clock was too much for Toby; he decided to let me do the tour and he would meet us at the museum. Somewhat incensed at hearing this, I suggested that perhaps he would prefer not to be with us at all. Oh no! He would love to lunch at the hotel because the food was the best in Boston. But he would meet us before lunch at the museum because it was necessary for me to get a view of some cultural values. He could point these out to my advantage, if not pleasure.

The couple turned out to be very pleasant company. I was driven through the streets of Roxburgh—the black quarter or ghetto—in a closed car. I got an indelible impression of squalor and ugliness. The houses once were dignified and gracious, lived in by families with servants. Now they are dirty and crumbling, let out in rooms, decrepit and seamy. No wonder there is violence there. Every street corner had teenagers standing around, listless and apathetic. Everywhere there were swarms of very young children. Then I was shown the section where the wealthy now live. Such lovely homes and gardens! The contrast was painful to me; it must be even more so for the Negroes.

I really did enjoy the visit to the museum. It was an oasis of peace and harmony. Toby, who had already been round it twice before we arrived, proceeded to give me the benefit of his knowledge. The pictures *he* thought were 'exquisite'—privately I thought were dull and dreary. Toby seems to yearn for anything that is the apotheosis of gloom.

Most museums are lavish in their architecture and magnificent in their possessions; but it is always an exhausting process trying to see as many of the exhibits as possible. The Isabella Stewart Garden Museum is just the right size. It is the house where this American lady lived and collected all her treasures over a fairly long life. There are rooms all round a beautiful courtyard with a sunken garden. Even I, who am no great lover of nature, stood to admire this small oasis of beauty.

The tapestries were marvels of fine and patient workmanship, but the main exhibits are pictures—pictures that I can understand, not pop art. What a tremendous amount of money and time went to assemble the collection! Americans are often said to be a very materialistic race, with few aesthetic values, but love and good taste as well as money had furnished this house.

We lunched at the Ritz-Carlton, in lush opulent surroundings —blue chandeliers, lofty ceilings and gold paint. There were three members of the Church at the next table looking well-fed and complacent. After their lunch they drank liqueurs and smoked cigarettes in long holders. Maybe they were full of care and concern for the poverty-stricken, but if so it didn't affect their appetites. I couldn't help feeling that the Ritz-Carlton was not exactly the right environment for those whose profession is saving souls.

I must say I did enjoy my lunch: good food, wine and conversation, an irresistible combination. I started with the pâté, which was just right, soft enough to spread but not gooey. Then I had lobster thermidor, one of my favourite dishes. Not knowing much about wine, I don't know what we drank; I do know that it enhanced the meal considerably.

After the lunch with our new-found friends we went to their home; they lived in a place called Ipswich. Some of this was a perfect example of a Puritan village, with houses made of clapboard, many of them with plaques bearing the year that they were built, round about 1700. The government will not allow these old Puritan houses to be altered. But they were in such a well-preserved condition, that I did wonder if they were the originals. It does seem a long time for wooden houses to last.

We were taken to see a large mansion built in the English style a long time ago by an American millionaire. He had visions of entertaining distinguished guests there, perhaps even royalty; but they never came. The house was in perfect taste, with a long sweep of lawn in front stretching a mile ahead. It reminded me of the drive that the Queen takes from Windsor to the races. The millionaire made his money from plumbing-equipment—baths, sinks and lavatories—not the kind of thing that one associates with our landed gentry. But to be a wealthy American was not synonymous with vulgarity, even all those years back.

Our friends' home had originally started as a fairly small one, but over the years more and more had been added on—and up, so that now it had seven bedrooms and five bathrooms. Yet still it was one of the most home-like houses I have ever been in. But with all those added rooms it must be a nightmare to clean. One tends to believe that Americans just wouldn't live in an old rambling, inconvenient house, away from the town; but that's another fallacy. I could tell that this house was loved. I said goodbye to these charming people with real regret.

Toby decided that we should go down to the waterfront to see the famous old ship that was moored in the Navy Yard; the U.S.S. *Constitution*. Naturally, as Toby was coming, we went by taxi, and the driver, finding that I was English, said that he had never been to Europe. For the moment I wondered what that had to do with me. I never feel that England belongs to Europe; we are just us. Europe is where those foreigners live—the Dutch, French, Belgians and Germans. Of course, now we're in the Common Market, I suppose we are just another state of Europe.

The nickname of this old ship is 'Old Ironsides'. When I enquired of Toby why was it called this, he loftily explained that the ship was so invincible that cannon-balls bounced off the deck. This old frigate had fought forty-four battles and won them all: against pirates in the West Indies; on the shores of Tripoli in 1803; and great naval victories in the War of 1812; and every rating had done his duty without thought of self. I discovered afterwards that Toby had acquired all this knowledge from a postcard on sale in the hotel.

Why we had to visit the ship was a mystery to me as I was sure that Toby's knowledge of the sea was limited to flying over it, and he wouldn't know how to tread the deck if he tried. I think that he wanted to demonstrate how quickly he could get up and down those steep steps that led to the depths—I practically stunned myself when I tried. To be honest it was well worth the journey. Down below, the ceiling was so low that anybody over five feet three inches had to stoop—were the sailors so short? I reckon the cook must have performed marvels of ingenuity to cook for a ship's crew in his tiny little kitchen. The whole ceiling of the lower deck was lined with shiny red life-preservers; I earmarked the one that was going to save me—if the polluted water didn't finish me off first. When I too read of the victories of this ship, I could realize why the American people were so proud of her.

Cambridge is a very pleasant part of Boston; it seems to have a sense of history. It's full of museums, art galleries and old attractive houses. And, of course, it has Harvard University, the oldest university in the United States.

Boston University has some hideous Victorian-type houses, and along the river are enormous square blocks, but Harvard seemed very pleasant amid the trees and lawns. I would have loved to be able to see inside some of the buildings, if only to compare them with some of our universities. I did notice a 'fall-out' shelter for use in the event of an atom bomb being dropped; but as obviously it could hold only a certain number of people, I couldn't help wondering how the favoured few would be selected. What would be the criterion of their eligibility?

We went into Harvard Museum to see the famous glass flowers, but as is the case with most museums, the exhibits are so profuse that one rushes madly from case to case to take everything in, and ends up by seeing nothing thoroughly. I was fascinated by a model of a gold nugget that, when it was originally dug out of the rock, was worth £41,000; I should think that if it had been a real nugget it would be worth untold wealth by now. But then they would never dare to keep it in the museum without an armed guard in attendance.

Some of the houses looked very odd, with very small windows at the top. I learned that this was because the British taxed the Americans on the number of storeys their houses had; so they built them with half-storeys at the top to escape the tax.

Our journey ended with a drive to see the house where Longfellow lived and the memorial to Mary Baker Eddy, both of which I would cheerfully have missed. I was put off Longfellow for life by having to learn *Hiawatha* at school, and recite it to the class, to the accompaniment of giggles every time I had to say Minnehaha. As for Mary Baker Eddy, I never could or would believe in a religion that denies the reality of illness and pain, or claims that these can be cured by prayer.

I was looking forward to seeing New York, as I had heard so much about it, not all complimentary, from Americans in England. All I knew of New York was the one night that I spent in the Manhattan Hotel last year, as one of the guests on a David Frost programme. I was warned not to leave the hotel in the evening to wander the streets. As, reading in my bedroom, I heard what was either several cars back-firing or revolver shots, I experienced no urge to venture into the unknown.

Nevertheless, I enjoyed Boston. How could I not? It was my first experience of American life. I had landed here with a feeling that Boston would mean nothing to me, perhaps because, prior to leaving England, I constantly heard, 'You will love Boston; it's so much like England.' I couldn't see the point in travelling three thousand miles to find a place just like the one that I had left behind. But Boston had charmed me, perhaps because some of it was reminiscent of a life that is gone for ever. I particularly remember Beacon Hill with its fascinating old brownstone houses, some all *art nouveau*, with cobbled pavements of red bricks, and arched doorways. Indeed I was reminded of a more gracious age.

In the plane I experienced my usual feeling of apprehension as we tore down the runway in case it wasn't long enough. If only I could sit with the captain to see just how much length he had left! Toby was kind enough to hold my hand and told me not to worry. Though why do people think that you can cease from worrying on their say-so? It's easy for him, as, if he is to be believed, a great part of his life seems to have been devoted to dashing around the world. One flight more or less made no difference.

3: New York

I was in a fever of excitement at the thought of seeing New York. To tell my family that I had been to Boston, Washington, or even the Grand Canyon, would arouse only luke-warm interest; but New York—that was really something.

Coming up the Hudson River and seeing the skyline of New York from the plane was out of this world, more like something from science fiction. All those towers, pinnacles, square blocks soaring to heaven; from the plane the buildings seemed to touch the clouds. It was as though I was viewing a Grimms'-fairy-tale land of castles. As it was evening, lights were on in all those marvellous sky-scrapers; it seemed the heavens were lit up to welcome me. I wanted to talk and talk, to share all this excitement—with somebody like me who had never seen it, or ever thought they'd be so lucky.

I was sure that I was going to love the city. Fancy, to think that in no time at all I would be walking on those streets, among New Yorkers, one of that great mass of *real* Americans. Who would have thought it could happen to me? If only some of my ex-employers could see me now! I just couldn't wait to get out and sample some of the life. But as it was so late I couldn't walk around—at least Toby said I couldn't, unless I wanted to leave New York almost as soon as entering it—and permanently.

The following day was a Sunday; and as I knew it would be all of ten o'clock before Toby appeared, I couldn't wait for him, I was so dead keen to savour New York.

I expected to find a Sunday comparable to a Sunday in London, rather empty and quiet, with what cars there were about all intent on driving out of the city. Nothing of the kind. New York seemed to be jam-packed with people and traffic, and as noisy as a weekday in Oxford Street. I like to hear the noise of a city; it's life being lived. There were young people in a long procession marching up and down with banners that proclaimed their solidarity with Soviet Jewry. Looking at this motley collection of youth, whose attire must surely have come from all the jumble sales that ever were, made me feel certain that this shouting and marching wouldn't make one iota of difference to the Kremlin. On the other hand, one can think it admirable that young people do care enough to protest against injustice. I said as much to a dour and elderly man standing next to me. 'In England, on a Sunday, all these people would be speaking in Hyde Park,' I told him, thinking, in a somewhat big-headed way that he would be interested to hear an English voice. He took not the slightest notice of my so-called Cockney accent.

'Do you know what this lot is?' he said angrily. 'It's the army of the great unwashed, under-privileged majority. Just look at them; never done a decent day's work in their lives. As for their bloody hair, if I had my way I'd take the garden-shears to the lot of them. If they are so fond of the goddamn Jews in Russia, why don't they just get out there and join them?'

When I told him that we had just the same problem back in England, he became, if that was possible, even gloomier. 'I'd send the goddamn lot to Vietnam. Let them see what misery really is; maybe they wouldn't shout about rights.' He, and as I found later on, a great many of his generation, equated the good all-American boys with close-cropped hair, formal dress and life-style conforming. Any deviation from this labelled them as loud-mouthed, good-for-nothing thugs. To listen to this vituperation was sad, and terrifying, because it was unreasoning.

It seems as though cleanliness is more than godliness. But it wasn't always, as a young friend of mine found out during the last World War. She fell in love with one of those very handsome Americans in the Air Force—it was that lovely uniform that did it—who looked the personification of every mother's darling, from a male edition of *Little Women*. To me, these types were always suspect, inasmuch as, allied to good looks, they were a walking gold-mine compared with English soldiers; so girls flocked around them in droves. My friend Mary met this Merle at a dance and fell for him hook, line and sinker. In vain did I urge her to find out more about him before committing herself. All that happened was that I nearly lost a friend. Eventually she got pregnant, found out he was already married and never got a penny out of him. What a lovely all-American boy he was!

I managed to tear myself away from this teeming street in case Toby was getting worried at my absence—one can always hope.

In New York neither he nor I were in a hotel. He was on one side of the city, staying with friends; this was fine for him; he was living in congenial company. But I was right on the other side of New York, in an apartment belonging to some absent friends of Toby's. I bet if he were in Lapland he'd have friends in the next igloo. It was a very pleasant apartment, luxurious even, but so high up that it was as quiet as the grave, and, on that first evening, about as welcoming. My only lifeline was the telephone to where Toby was staying; and when he left me, I got a strong impression of 'Don't ring me, I'll ring you.' He justified this arrangement on the grounds that we would be saving money. I'd far sooner have not been economical. At least in a hotel I could have gone into the bar and realized I was still alive.

As soon as Toby came over he produced a long list of things I ought to see and do, starting off with the Metropolitan Museum. I wasn't dismayed, for I felt so full of energy and enthusiasm I could have done anything—given the opportunity, of course.

The first thing I did was to take a taxi to the Metropolitan Museum. It was my first experience of travelling in a New York taxi, and I honestly thought it would be my last. It seemed to me that I literally took my life in my hands. The drivers are compelled to drive in a mad way because if they are two seconds late in pulling away from the lights, all the traffic behind them starts hooting like the trumpet brigade. I know, because we were three seconds late, and I thought a brass band was behind us. New York taxis are not a patch on our London ones. Never have I seen so many battered vehicles with their backs stove in. One driver told me it's not worth having the car repaired. It costs too much; it's cheaper to buy another one. Most of the taxis are very dirty by our standards, neither do ours have to have a bullet-proof sheet of Perspex between the driver and passenger. There is a notice to the effect that the driver cannot change more than five dollars; the fare goes into a locked box and he hasn't the key. So if the driver gets held-up by a gun, the robbers have to pull the whole cash-box away from the taxi. I found that most of the drivers were nice to me; they seemed to think that I was a Cockney, so I put the accent on even more. A Mr Joe Evans drove me in one of the few taxis in which one could talk to the driver. Mind you, it would need to be a tough customer who would attack Mr Joe Evans. He told me that he went in for weight-lifting, to develop his muscles. Certainly, if those bulging lumps of flesh were his muscles he had done a real good job with the development. As for his chest, it looked as though a goodly portion of the Amazonian jungle had settled there. He told me that he was one of nine sons and his ma was still going strong family-wise. Well, as he said, it's a way of passing the evening. Fancy having nine boys. I'd have gone crackers. Even after three babies, the monotony of one sex was getting me down. I know it's a fifty-fifty chance, but just imagine if I'd kept on trying to have a girl, and ended up with nine males—absolutely demoralizing! When I got out of the taxi Joe Evans invited me to feel his muscles. I can't say that I was wildly enthusiastic to do this in a crowded street. On the other hand, no London taxi-driver has ever asked me to feel his muscles—though I have been asked to do other things. Joe is coming to London next year; he wants to marry an English girl, one who can cook. I have invited him to call on me. I just hope that he doesn't think the invitation includes his eight brothers!

By the time I had prodded Joe's biceps and said farewell, I could see that the museum was going to be 'done' at the gallop. The Metropolitan is an enormous building, with the main entrance on Fifth Avenue. When I entered what is called the Great Hall, and saw how huge the place was, with galleries leading off in all directions, I knew that one would need the constitution of an ox to traipse up and down that lot, as well as winged feet. I felt even more despondent on reading the catalogue. So many thousands of pictures and drawings: there were 4,000 objects of medieval art alone. What hopes had I of seeing a tithe of it in the limited time available to me?

Entrance to the Metropolitan is, in theory, free, but there is a notice inviting you to pay what you like to help support this cultural collection. Human nature being what it is they know that a great many people would pay only a dime. So they suggest that adults pay a minimum of a dollar and children half that. As a dollar is about eight shillings, it's not exactly a cheap outing if you have a family. Needless to say, I paid the minimum. After all, back in England, where I am frequently a visitor to museums, I shall have to help support them now that they are charging a fee.

Inwardly muttering a few uncomplimentary remarks about Joe Evans for delaying me, I decided to spend most of my available time in the American wing. After all, I was supposed to be discovering America; I reckoned that included the past. Anyway, that's what I intended to tell Toby if he complained, as undoubtedly he would, that being second nature to him.

One tends to think of America as a place new and modern, with every labour-saving gadget and device that has ever been invented. So it was rather fascinating to look at all this old colonial way of life, in such sharp contrast to the American way of life now. (I once read in an American magazine that in the home there is electrical equipment for every conceivable household task. All I can say is, if these gadgets break down as often as ours do, an American housewife's time must often be devoted to carting all this stuff back to the shop to be repaired. Or do they just throw them out with the garbage? They are supposed to follow the cult of obsolescence.) To my surprise I really did enjoy looking at the bygone aspect of America. One of the most interesting exhibits was the reconstituted Assembly Rooms from Gadsby Tavern, Virginia, with a huge pair of brick chimneys, Queen Anne chairs and brass chandeliers. It was here that George Washington attended his last birthday ball in 1789. Most of the exhibits seemed to have come from the New England State of Massachusetts.

Having done my duty nobly by inspecting all this past glory of America, I felt justified in rushing to spend a few minutes with my favourite, the Egyptian room; given the time I could stay for hours. I'm fascinated to think of those Pharaohs dying with all their worldly goods around them, ready for the next life. Obviously they had never known that you can't take it with you.

I did try to find a minute to see the painting that cost the museum 2,300,000 dollars. This is Rembrandt's 'Aristotle Contemplating the Bust of Homer', but after walking what seemed like a couple of miles I gave up, and decided to contemplate the 'Contemplation' on another day.

I joined the crowd that was watching a demonstration of Chinese calligraphy; this was really beautiful. On some half-dozen television screens the characters were traced out and the meaning of them explained. The writing was more like a work of art than mere words; it was the only writing that I have ever seen that had aesthetic value.

Two hours of the museum was enough for one day; besides, I wanted to walk in Central Park. Toby had said that it was safe to do this in the daylight. It was certainly a huge place, 840 acres in all. As my feet were killing me by now I sat on a bench and watched the fashions. Perhaps Central Park, unlike Hyde Park, is not a fashion-conscious place. Some of the middle-aged, broad-in-the-beam American ladies in trousers had to be seen to be believed. The colours shrieked to heaven and the seams appeared to be bursting apart—the back view was even more hilarious than the front.

I strolled by the lake which really looked pretty with daffodils all around. But when I came back there half an hour later, I was astonished to find that all the daffodils had disappeared. Children and adults had picked them by the armful to take home. I don't think that Wordsworth would have received inspiration to write his poem here.

In spite of the crowds of people in the park, squirrels were running up and down the trees and eating nuts that people threw to them. It was difficult to visualize violence here, but not many people venture in to the park when it gets dark. Not that I had any intention of walking there in the evening. I had my share of that kind of thing when I was young and searching for a young man with honourable intentions. In pairs we would roam around Hyde Park with our eyes wide open for any 'possibles'.

As I had foreseen, Toby wasn't in the least impressed with all I had done in the way of sight-seeing; he thought it a very poor showing, and almost a day wasted. On my enquiring what *he* had done, all I got in reply was, 'That's nothing to do with it. You're not here to enjoy yourself; you are here to write a book.' I believe that he considers I turn books out on a conveyor-belt.

So, on the next morning—and I am convinced that he occasionally has sadistic tendencies—Toby told me that, as part of my education in sight-seeing, I would definitely have to go to the top of the Empire State Building; all 102 storeys of it, or 1,860 steps if you prefer to walk up. He said that nobody, just nobody, visited New York without going to the top of the building. I actually believed this at the time—there's one born every minute. The prospect of doing this filled me with alarm and absolute terror, for I suffer from vertigo, so much so, that if I am in a building higher than the fifth floor I never go near the window. In vain I pointed out to Toby that I might be able to claim some measure of fame by being the first visitor *not* to go to the top of the Empire State Building; he was not impressed at my creating a record. Anyway, I flatly refused to attempt this feat without imbibing some Dutch courage, so he had to buy me two large brandies first. Even then, in the lift I was speechless with fright—and it takes a lot to make me speechless. What if the lift broke down halfway? Besides, I had been told that on a windy day the building sways as much as four inches, and this was a windy day. The journey up seemed never-ending.

I'm willing to believe that the view from the top is breath-taking, if one only had the courage to look at it—I didn't. I bet nobody has been around the top of that building quicker than me. One of the drawbacks of American lifts is that they descend so suddenly and swiftly that you feel as though part of your anatomy has been left behind. And they will persist in calling them elevators.

Anyway, Toby got me up there under false pretences, for during my stay in New York I talked to people, visitors and residents, who not only had never been to the top of the Empire State Building, but were also firmly intending never to go, either. What sense, and how lucky they were to be able to do as they liked!

As we were going out to dinner in the evening I wanted to get my hair done. So I looked around for a hairdressing shop, one that looked as though they wouldn't charge the earth for doing the job. In some of these very elaborate establishments it seems that a pound is rung up as soon as you step on the mat. I found a place that looked pretty ordinary outside, but when I got inside I knew that I had made a mistake. It appeared to be exclusively staffed by men—well, I think they were men. One of them, who was wearing a pink frilly shirt and seemed to be enveloped in an invisible cloud of attar of something or other, stepped delicately up to me and said, 'What can I do for you?' I felt like replying, 'Very little by the look of you.' At the end, my hair wasn't done a bit better than they do it in Hove, so I nearly died when I got the bill for ten dollars. No wonder he could afford to buy pink frilly shirts and attar of—could it have been violets?

In the evening we went down to Chinatown for a real Chinese meal at a place recommended by a friend of Toby's. I was a bit taken aback when I got inside, as I had expected to see oriental décor, or at least something reminiscent of the mysterious East. This place wasn't reminiscent of anything at all, unless it was an English transport café. Was it for this I had spent a small fortune in the hairdressers'? A scarf tied round my head would have done here. However, the food was absolutely wonderful, the best Chinese food that I had ever eaten. Though to be honest, I hadn't eaten Chinese food more than twice in my life, so my opinion didn't count for much. I hadn't a clue what I was eating; perhaps it was as well. The only drawback was the chopsticks. I simply cannot manipulate these objects so that the food is caught between them. It always falls out. If I try to balance the food on the top of the two sticks it slides off before I can get it high enough to eat. What made it even more frustrating was that the diners around me were wielding these chopsticks as though to the manner born. In my opinion there's a lot to be said for using knives and forks; I'll never believe that the food doesn't taste the same.

We wandered around the Chinese quarter, very crowded, but very colourful. Whether it is naturally like that or whether they add the trimmings for tourists I don't know. There were bazaars, still open, and grocery shops with the strangest stock—dried squid, shark fins, and something floating around in a glass bottle that looked like a shrunken head—but I don't suppose it was.

Every now and again a Bowery bum, as they are called—but

not by me—would shuffle along the street. These wrecks of humanity come from the Bowery, or Skid Row. We walked down there but didn't stay long; it seemed to me too awful to stand and gaze at these derelicts as though they were exhibits—an invasion of their privacy. It's not dangerous to walk on the Bowery, but it's very depressing. The buildings are dirty, as are the hundreds or thousands who live there. They lie on the pavements, or in shop doorways, some clutching bottles of their usual drink, a mixture of rot-gut wine and cheap alcohol. The police just let them alone unless they become violent. There is a Bowery Mission that tries to help them, but it must be a hopeless job, not only because there are not enough helpers, or money, but because the derelicts don't want to be helped.

After this, Toby, with a complete disregard for my safety, and risking his valuable property—that's me—took me to the Italian quarter, or Mafia land. And not only into the quarter: he took me into the very place where the Mafia chief, Joe Gallo, was murdered on 7 April 1972. This was in Umberto's Clam House on Mulberry Street. I had simply no idea that we were anywhere near such a place; if I had known, wild horses wouldn't have dragged me in there. I was sitting with my back to the very same door through which entered the four racketeers who gunned down Joe Gallo. I read in the *New York Times* that Gallo and his bodyguard were sitting with their backs to the door. Well, wouldn't you have thought they'd have more sense? If I was living such a precarious life I'd always have my back to the wall. The report said also that 'at the first shots Gallo began to swear'. Can you blame him? I nearly did the same thing to Toby for having the nerve to take *me* there; why, I too might have got shot in the back. Toby said that the Mafia never shoot at women; but bullets can ricochet. If I had known that I was in Umberto's, every time I heard the door slam I'd have been under the table in a flash. I know that in the cause of science—is book-writing a science?—one has to make sacrifices. But not the supreme one! When it was pointed out to me what a tremendous amount of publicity I would receive if my body had to be shipped back to England—probably all my books would start to sell in America—I was not impressed.

'What about the one I am supposed to be here for, *Margaret*

39

Powell in America? How could I write it from the grave?'

'Oh, that would be a posthumous book. We would publicize it, "after Margaret Powell" '—I bet it would be a long way after, too—'It would sell like hot cakes. With some minuscule part of the profits we could keep your grave embellished with flowers.'

Big deal, what's the good of that if I can't smell them?

Toby was certainly keeping to his decision that I should 'do' New York thoroughly. Next morning there he was at the apartment again, complete with list. Next item, a Gray Line Bus Tour.

It took me some days to discover that he always found he was unable to accompany me on these tours because of pressure of business. He had to make or receive telephone calls, or call on somebody, always for my benefit of course. In the beginning, I really believed all these excuses, but then I hadn't known him for very long. Later, I realized that he heartily disliked bus tours. He couldn't stand the non-stop flow of information and badinage from the driver. Neither did he care to become one of a crocodile of passengers walking along exposed to the public gaze. Not for Toby 'solidarity with the masses'.

At first I felt somewhat indignant at being expected to do all this sight-seeing on my own; later on I preferred it. For dining and wining Toby was an ideal companion; but as a tourist he was hopeless.

This Gray Line Tour took four and a half hours. At the end of it I was stuffed so full of facts and figures that I felt I was as good as a walking encyclopaedia on the State of New York.

I had a young man of about eighteen years as my seat-mate; he was very shy at first and kept calling me ma'am all the time. Eventually I got fed up with this; it made me feel like a schoolmarm, so I persuaded him to call me Margaret. In the time he was on the bus we got very friendly. He came from Minnesota and was working on his father's farm and engaged to be married, too; but that was off. 'That's why I'm working in New York, to get away from seeing her.'

'Why did it end?' I asked sympathetically.

'Because she didn't like a farm-worker; she said there was no money in it.'

I wanted to say that there were as good fish in the sea as ever came out, but he didn't want his tragedy minimized; he wanted attention; so I concentrated on him. He wouldn't tell me his name at first, saying he couldn't 'stick to be known by it'. It turned out that his ma had him baptized Upton, after the American author, Upton Sinclair. By this time our driver was really getting into his stride; so fast and furious did the jokes pour out that I couldn't help but feel he had missed his vocation; he should have been on the stage. I said as much to Upton, meaning it to be a kind of joke, but he took me literally; he really thought I meant our driver was good enough for the stage. Well, as he made Upton fall about with laughing perhaps I have no sense of American humour.

We were shown the statue of Columbus, who discovered America, or so we were taught at school. I don't know why they have built a statue to him because he didn't even know he had reached America. Not only has he got immortality in stone; in some of the American states they also have a public holiday for him on 12 October. Why don't we have these events? What about a public holiday to commemorate Sir Francis Drake? Although when I mentioned this to Albert, all he could remember concerning him was that he played bowls. Talk about our glorious heritage!

Our next 'object of interest' in the tour was the Museum of Natural History, an absolute colossus of a building; one side of it looked like a medieval castle. They have the skeleton of a brontosaur which is supposed to have weighed thirty-five tons when it was alive. There is also a primate hall with the exhibits arranged in the order of the descent of man. Really, the more I examined them, the more I was convinced that some people have only just got off the trees. Not my friends, of course. I was really impressed by the huge department showing animals in their natural habitat.

Our guide round the museum was chiefly concerned to tell us the value of everything; that the whole collection in the museum was worth about forty million dollars. This is one of those meaningless statements that nobody can refute, because nobody knows whether or not it's true. But then our guide wasn't an official one, just one of those know-alls that you get on these bus tours. This particular one had travelled all the way from Washington, Virginia, by car, through all the New England states into New York state. He must have travelled through some wonderful little villages, and scenery; yet he seemed to have seen nothing, nor even wanted to. Roads were just a means of locomotion. The whole conversation in the bus was what freeways he had travelled on; how many miles he had been able to go in a day without stopping; and above all, how much the whole thing had cost him.

Fortunately, when we went into the Cathedral of St John, the immensity of the place over-awed even this man. It is said to be the largest Gothic cathedral in the world and can accommodate 10,000 worshippers at a time. I should never have thought that there would ever be so many people all going to church at the same time. It is a beautiful place, but to me it was, like so many other things in America, too over-powering—too much stained glass, too many columns, too much ornament.

We were taken to Brooklyn Bridge from which, or so our face-tious driver said, 'In the old days, people used to jump when they wanted to commit suicide. Now they jump off the Empire State Building to make sure of it.' A somewhat sour voice from the back of the bus was heard to comment, 'They needn't bother nowadays to do either. Just walk around New York at night and they will get it done without any effort on their part.'

Our driver still kept up his flow of fun and jokes. We had just passed a strip-tease, when he said, 'Do you know, there was a fire at that go-go place. It took an hour to put it out and two hours to put the firemen out.' Heavens, I thought, if only somebody would put you out!

Shortly after this, Upton said that he had had enough of sight-seeing, so he left the bus. I believe he felt rather embarrassed at telling me of the tragedy of his lost love and at the same time laughing his head off at the entertainer up front. I should have told him that even clowns can have a broken heart. This left me with nobody to talk to until a man of about fifty-five to sixty came and sat next to me, much to the fury of four elderly females who had been doing their utmost to get him into conversation. It's just no good hunting in packs; you have far more success on your own. A man feels that he can get away from one female—though he would have been lucky to get away from me—but four females is taking on too much. Why, he might have got killed in the crush—or rush. His name was Jack Mitchell and he came from Ottawa. He proceeded to tell me, at great length and detail, just why he was taking a holiday. His wife had died three months ago, and all his friends had told him that the best way to recover from the loss was to have a change of scene. I knew nothing of Ottawa, except that it was in Ontario; but even I could sense that New York was about the most complete change possible from what I had read of life in Canada. Jack Mitchell worked in a factory where they made paper from wood-pulp—or was it the other way round? As I got to know him more I couldn't help but feel that the reason they had urged him to take this trip was simply in the hopes that he might find another wife —and perhaps also because it was so far away. Anything to take him off their hands; for really, this Jack was an absolute non-stop talker, and the platitudes came popping out like peas from a pod, each one uttered as though it was a pearl of wisdom.

'My wife,' he said, 'was a jewel. I was twenty-five and she was ten years older when we got married, but I never thought that she would go before me. We just lived for each other; we didn't want or need children. She was a wife in a thousand, an absolute pearl. She listened to me, and loved to hear all my little jokes.'

To all this eulogy I kept on nodding my head like a mandarin and making suitable expressions of sympathy. Well, you've got to, when you've managed to snaffle the only unattached male on the bus. I don't reckon that's being a hypocrite. After all, I knew neither him nor his departed wife.

'How did your wife die? Was it an accident?' I eventually managed to ask.

'Nobody, not even the doctor, knows why. She just suddenly gave up going out with me, wouldn't eat, shut herself in the parlour, wouldn't speak to me, sat there day after day, then just died in good health.'

I wonder if it could have been through sheer boredom, perhaps in self-defence against the Niagara of talk.

By this time the bus had reached the ferry that was taking us across to Staten Island and the Statue of Liberty, or the Liberty Belle as some Americans called her. The tablet that she holds in her left hand is supposed to be emblematic of the Declaration of Independence, and at her feet are the chains of slavery, broken. This 151-foot national monument was the idea of the French historian and admirer of the American way of life, Edouard de

Laboulaye. He suggested that the French present it to the United States as a token of their esteem. The U.S. finally got it in 1885. Why they couldn't give us one too I don't know. I'm sure we could have found somewhere to put it—Piccadilly perhaps? And I reckon that our political system is every bit as good as in America, if not better. But perhaps *we* weren't esteemed by the French at that time.

My loquacious friend Jack was *very* attentive going over on the ferry. He fought his way through the crush to get me an orangeade. I ask you! An orangeade! How exciting! It did nothing for me. I half-thought of losing him, as I was sure getting fed up with a detailed account of his marital life. But prestige was at stake; I couldn't let the four females take him over. I even promised to have dinner with him in his hotel.

The idea when we got to Staten Island was to ascend right to the top of the statue; not from the outside of course—or I would never have left the boat. The only perils I could contend with would be the 'perils of Pauline'. The statue really did look impressive the closer we came. Once it had been shiny copper, but the weather has coated it with a green verdigris. The torch alone is supposed to be large enough to hold twelve people—not that it ever has, at that height, to my knowledge. An elevator takes you up to one observation platform, but if you want to go right to the top you have to climb a narrow spiral stairway of 168 steps, with nothing but a kind of wire mesh between you and what seems like New York. In the normal way nothing would have induced me to attempt such a hazardous feat, but my friend from Ottawa urged me to do it.

'I'll be right behind you to see that you are all right. You trust in me. If I can do it, you can too.'

Even then I might have refused, but, to the accompaniment of girlish laughter, the four veteran ladies said that they were going right to the top. 'Aren't we brave? Who will rescue us if we get nervous?'

You can bet your life it won't be Jack Mitchell, I muttered under my breath; I'll make sure he'll be too busy looking after me. Well, I have never been so mistaken in a man as I was with that Jack. All that sad monologue on the bus seemed as though it never was. Talk about helping me up the stairs; he practically lifted me up them. His idea of assistance seemed to mean holding me round the waist with one hand while the other was on my ankles. Well, it started off on my ankles. Thank heavens I was wearing tights. I haven't ever given the matter much thought, but the wearing of tights must surely be somewhat frustrating to some men—passion-coolers perhaps. But on this staircase they were indispensable—not that *I* needed a passion-cooler.

I must say, that after reaching the top, it was well worth the trouble; one could see for miles. As the observation platform was covered in, I wasn't too nervous, though it was 260 feet above sea-level.

Now I look back on it, going back in that bus was really funny, Jack had completely changed. Not a word did I hear about his dear departed. All I got was a detailed account of his one-time sexual exploits—and if we hadn't been on a bus I believe he would have given a practical demonstration. In fact so amorous did he become that any idea of having dinner with him rapidly left me. If I had to hold his hand on the bus, I could easily imagine how it would be in a more private situation. Talk about 'after the feast, comes the reckoning'! Did I encourage him? No, I'm sure that I didn't.

At two-thirty I staggered into the apartment, only to find Toby there, full of ideas as to the next item on the list. I didn't realize that New York was to be an endurance test. This time it was to visit a small private museum, the Frick Collection. He was coming too; he can always find time when it is something that really interests him; in this case the old masters. The collection is housed in what once was the home of Henry Clay Frick, a steel baron. It took him over forty years to acquire all the lovely things, with the help of another great collector, Andrew Mellon; then he presented it to the nation. There are beautiful painted enamels of Limoges; Italian and French bronzes; old French furniture; and lovely decorative panels by Fragonard. The collection is all on one floor; one can walk around without getting exhausted or overwhelmed because there is too much. Above all, there are the old masters, Dutch, Italian, French and British. The only picture that I coveted was a Titian, 'Portrait of a Man in a Red Cap'; the expression and colouring were marvellous. Toby, who seems to know more about everything than I would have thought possible in his short lifetime, spent all his time in front of these paintings. I left him to it in case he asked me questions that I wouldn't have a clue how to answer.

To compensate for all my hard work on New York he was taking me to see a publisher the next day.

We have seen the publisher; he was a charming man. But then charm is a publisher's stock-in-trade. With it he welcomes best-selling authors, keeps possible best-sellers happy and manages to refuse the rubbish without offending would-be authors.

Unfortunately, this publisher showed no enthusiasm for me as an author for the great American public. Well, as he already has hundreds of authors on his list I suppose one can't blame him. If I could outdo some of the sexy books, I too might have got on his list. But as half of the things that they do in these books is a mystery to me—even that they know how to do them—I would never be able to think of anything fresh to say on the subject. It was never after-dinner conversation when I was young. I could think of the titles; the rest would be blank pages. Well, you'd have to use your imagination. There seem to be as many varieties of sexual warfare as of Heinz, and certainly a lot of stamina must be needed. Probably the end result is just the same; it's merely a way of passing the time.

To console me for my quick demise as an American literary success, Toby took me to a German restaurant for lunch; the first time I have eaten in one. Very good it was, too. There are restaurants to suit every nationality in New York: Chinese, Japanese, French, German and English, and many more. In this place all the staff were men and they actually smiled as they waited on us. In fact, our waiter had such a round, red and smiling face that I thought any minute he would burst forth with a German drinking song. Perhaps he did in the evening. I ate a fish called shad, though I admit that I was somewhat disconcerted to find that my portion of shad consisted only of roe. It was a large lump too. A shad must be a very fertile fish, judging by the number of eggs that I consumed. Well, like the salmon, it ascends rivers to spawn, so perhaps it was just going up one before I got it on my plate.

After lunch, to my surprise and relief, nothing had been arranged for me until the evening. Then we were meeting friends of Toby's in the King Cole Bar at the St Regis Hotel. I assumed that the bar was named after King Cole, of merry monarch fame; if so it was a misnomer. It was more like a mausoleum, full only of emptiness and quiet. Perhaps we were there too early. Nevertheless, I'll always remember that evening; it was a somewhat traumatic occasion for me. In addition to the normal drinks, Toby and his friends got me to consume three glasses of Mexican tequila. Never again; the results of drinking it were too drastic. My head felt as though it had expanded to three times its normal size. Alone in that apartment high above the ground I stood at the window, lord of all I surveyed. I imagined that if I undid the catch and let in the night, I could fly out on wings. I still don't know what kept me from trying. It was one of the worst experiences of my life. As far as I am concerned, Mexico can keep its native spirit. Fortunately, by the next morning all was well.

I was out and about so often that I decided I needed to buy a dress. So I went into the enormous store called Bloomingdales. I was prepared to spend a reasonable amount of money, but finished up by spending nothing. First, because I discovered that I couldn't buy anything on the strength of an American Express card. This was something of a shock to me, as, reading the glowing accounts of the inestimable benefits that ensue from owning an American Express card, I was naturally somewhat astonished to find that this huge store refused it. I was informed that they have their own system of credit cards. Why only theirs? Don't they trust other systems? One very nice and helpful assistant took time off from serving customers to try to explain the reasons, but I'm afraid that I understood only one word in ten; something about Bloomingdales being large enough to adopt their own credit cards, which were simpler than those of other concerns. But secondly, I think that I would have bought very little because the sheer size of the establishment is daunting to a stranger; I walked and walked. Any department that I wanted seemed to be miles removed from the one that I was already in. Of course, the regular customers have worked out the topography and take all the short cuts.

As though I hadn't trudged around enough in Bloomingdales,

I bought an official map of a walking tour of downtown New York. All the time, when one hears New York mentioned, it is a city modern and teeming with life. So I was interested to read in the guide that New York was originally New Amsterdam, founded by the Dutch in 1624. The British took it over, with no opposition, in 1664 and renamed it in honour of the Duke of York.

The sun was shining and the buildings were *not* ugly. I have seen many more beautiful modern buildings in America than ever I have back home. For America has everything in abundance: labour, material and land on which to build. Instead of patching up the old, they rebuild, and they do it well, practically and aesthetically.

I walked down the long, straight streets, like man-made canyons, with just a square of blue sky at the end of the long vista. If I half-closed my eyes I could imagine that these towering blocks were cliffs, escarpments and mountains. But in the midst of nature's wonders, I feel diminished, insignificant, a nobody: here I really felt ten feet tall, among all these marvels made by man.

I wandered into Trinity Church, completed in 1846. In the churchyard lies Robert Fulton, inventor of the steam-boat. I met there an American couple, who were also wandering around with the official guide-book. Mr and Mrs V. A. Butterworth were from just outside New York, and how very pleasant it was to have their company. They had lived in New York itself for ten years, but had never seen so much of it as they did now, just having a day's sight-seeing: just like Albert and me when we have a few days in London.

Mr Butterworth's hobby, now that he had retired, was collecting facts, pictures and anecdotes about old New York. So as we wandered through Manhattan I listened to a fascinating account of the island, right back to when a man called Peter Minuit bought it from the Indians for twenty-four dollars worth of trinkets and a barrel of rum. They must have drunk the rum first before they gave the land to him. Now, although Manhattan is only twelve miles long by two and a half miles wide, two million people live on it, with another three million coming in to work every day. Mr Butterworth is trying to write a book about all this past history; I do so hope he succeeds.

I returned from the expedition somewhat exhausted with all that walking. I did have an idea that this diligence would evoke a few words of commendation from Toby; but his response was only, 'Well, what of it? You're not here just to enjoy yourself.' Talk about devastating! I shall definitely give up trying to please. With great magnanimity I forbore to enquire, 'For what reason are *you* here?'

Today, 2 May, Edgar Hoover died. In the afternoon I was sitting in a self-service café drinking coffee, when the news came through. I was astonished to see several very respectable-looking people stand up and cheer.

'Now we can breathe again,' one of the men remarked.

That this feeling wasn't universal was shown by some of the customers, builders by the look of them, making angry noises in the direction of the cheerers.

Later on, Toby and I went to a literary party in Greenwich Village. The house was one of a very attractive row of terraced houses, all with wrought-iron work, rather flat windows and steps leading up to very wide doors. All the houses faced an avenue of trees, very pleasant indeed. One of the guests told me that the trees were gingko trees and that in Japan they are holy trees. She added that there are male and female gingko trees, and they are planted fairly close together so that they experience no difficulty when they get the urge to perpetuate their species. She didn't smile when she told me all this botany stuff but I still wonder if it's true.

But at this literary party there also seemed to be nothing but rejoicing at the news of Hoover's death, and that a repressive era was over. Not being well-versed in American politics—lord knows our own are complex enough since the advent of the Common Market—I asked why, if he were so much hated, he had been able to keep in office for so long.

'Because he knew so many secrets about those in high office,' I was told. 'So many skeletons in the cupboard in other people's lives. And this is how it was,' my informant went on; 'if Hoover thought that any official might have derogatory ideas about him, or even more if the official had actually uttered derogatory remarks at some party, he always knew because he had so many toadies in high places. He would telephone this individual, all unctuous and benevolent and say to him, "Charlie, I'd like to have a talk with you." Charlie, whose whole life was without secrets, couldn't see what harm Hoover could do him. But during the course of conversation, Hoover would let drop something quietly, like this: "Pity about your grandfather," or it might be nephew or cousin. Hoover had knowledge of something shocking that they had done in the past, something that Charlie had never suspected. "But, of course, old man," Hoover would add, "this is just between you and me." And another voice was silenced.'

But I got the opposite view going back to the apartment in a taxi. The taxi-driver, who was Irish, said to me, 'What do you think of the death of that Grand Old Man?' At first I was nonplussed. The only Grand Old Man that I could think of was Gladstone. I thought that Mr Mullins could hardly mean him; he'd been dead for years. Moreover, to the Irish, Gladstone was never an object of veneration. But suddenly it occurred to me that Mr Mullins meant Hoover. So, although I had so recently been listening to execrations of him, I thought it as well to be diplomatic. I didn't want to get turfed out of this taxi.

'Well, I'm British,' I said, cautiously, 'and have been here only a few days. Also I don't know much about Mr Edgar Hoover. The only Hoover I know is the one who was a President.'

'*He* was no goddamn good in the Depression,' Mr Mullins spat out. 'Edgar was the man for this country. America will break apart now. There's no one can take his place, or do what he's done. He kept under the goddamn Reds and the Mafia'—what about Joe Gallo, I thought—'he could smell them out like a goddamn dog can scent a fox.'

When I somewhat timidly remarked that not everybody seemed to be of his opinion, Mr Mullins was very quick to reply, 'All the goddamn people I know are.' Probably they wouldn't dare not to be; I know that I didn't.

I have read, and heard, that New York taxi-drivers are given to voicing philosophical views on life. I certainly missed out on this, riding with that brawny Mr Mullins.

Toby, who, I felt convinced, had already arranged an evening's delight that excluded me, introduced me to a really charming friend of his. This friend, Alec, on hearing that I had never been to a Greek restaurant, offered to take me. What a lovely idea, I thought. If there is one thing that I like more than anything else, it's being taken out to a meal by a man. I don't mind if they are young or old, though naturally, some are better than others. some older men can be perfect companions. They look after you as though you were some exotic plant that needed tender care. They pay such nice compliments, on your looks or your dress. Well, of course, they have had years of practice. Mind you, it's possible to be caught by one who uses you as a listening post. He will relate everything that goes wrong at work—never his fault. Or he will say that his wife doesn't understand him, when the truth is, she understands him only too well. Worst of all is the man who assures you that, 'A man is as old as he feels.' This is seldom true. He is generally as old as he is, and sometimes a sight older. This type will take you to dine where there is a dance-floor about the size of a pocket-handkerchief, and all through the meal he will forcibly remove you from the delights of the food to keep on jigging around. He generally holds you so tightly that you couldn't get a hair between you and him. On the other hand, most young men merely want to talk about love as an abstract thing, though I suspect they are very concrete when the opportunity arises. Well, that's all right with me; I can theorize about love until the cows come home. It's a lot safer and far less strenuous.

Anyway, this lovely, good-looking Alec took me to a Greek restaurant called Dionysos, on East 48th Street. Just fancy, in New York where I was completely unknown, to dine out in style with the right companion! Talk about fringe benefits: I'd got them all. Alec was known here, so we were greeted like old friends, and I was given a red rose, and a lot of smiles; so the atmosphere here was just how I liked it to be. It was a bonus to be taken out by such an attractive man and it was a super bonus to find that the staff welcomed him; I felt like royalty. Alec was determined that I should try as many Greek hors d'oeuvres as possible. He said that they act as an aphrodisiac. I wouldn't have thought that *he* needed one, and as for me, what would be the good of it with Albert over three thousand miles away? It's not even as though he has extra-sensory perception. Besides, I have found that aphrodisiacs have a tendency to make you feel loving towards the

wrong person; or in fact anybody who 'has it with him'. I must
say the hors d'oeuvres were delicious. Minute portions of spinach-
pie—sounds revolting but it wasn't; a piece of squid, such a thin
piece that it must have been the very end of one of its tentacles—
and I do mean *tentacles*—in spite of Alec's information about its
aphrodisiac qualities. There were also some mysterious small objects about the size of a walnut. I forbore to ask Alec what they
were, in case I got put off them. I ate everything, but then I
always do—a throwback to the time when I never knew where
the next meal was coming from.

It was a surprise to see a card on the table, 'Music Charge $2.50
per person'. You had to pay this whether you wanted the music
or not. 'I'm not a great lover of music,' I said to Alec, 'so ask
them to bring cotton-wool to stuff in my ears; then you needn't
pay for my share.'

Still, the Greek band did add to the gaiety of the evening,
especially when to my astonishment the Greek waiters linked
hands and danced in a circle with customers joining in whenever
they felt like doing so.

By this time, whether it was the hors d'oeuvres or the Greek
wine—probably the latter—I felt just like putting the rose between my teeth and doing a Carmen. Luckily for Alec I resisted
the impulse. I didn't want the dream to turn into a nightmare.

I reckon that this Greek restaurant was the gayest and liveliest I
had seen up to now. Instead of bored-looking dancers eternally
gyrating, the customers here got up and joined hands with anybody on the floor. They danced all through the restaurant and
round the tables, laughing and singing all the time.

Not only was there delicious Greek food but also what I
thought was real Greek atmosphere too. I felt so exhilarated
when we finally left that I could have gone on for hours. But
Alec, who was a personnel director in a hospital, was on duty
early the next morning; so as it was already midnight we had to
part. I was in such a euphoric state that I mentally forgave Toby
for all his misdeeds—it didn't last though.

On my last day in New York I was out of the apartment by
7.15 a.m. to have coffee and talk to a man about Queen Victoria.
He asked me not to put his name in my book so I'll call him
John. The previous day I had gone into his shop to buy some ball-

point pens. As soon as he heard my voice, he said, 'You come from the East End of London; I can always tell a Cockney.' I didn't disillusion him. Who was I to deliver such a blow to his pride by telling him that I was born in Sussex? John was about sixty years old, and he told me that his grandfather had been born in Scotland, had come to America when he was only eighteen, and married an Italian girl. He was very proud of his British ancestry, and when I told him that my mother had actually *seen* Queen Victoria in the flesh, he wanted to know all about it. He loved to read everything about that period. 'Could I possibly find the time to have a chat with him?'

How could I refuse such British patriotism?

So at 7.30 a.m. I was at the shop, sitting in the back-room drinking coffee with John and Queen Victoria. I hadn't the heart to tell him that my mother couldn't care less about the Queen when she was alive and by now had completely forgotten her existence. My mum's constant monologue used to start, 'She never did anything for me.' Fortunately, as I am studying history I am fairly well versed in that period and could keep John happy for an hour. I've often kept people happy for an hour, but never with Queen Victoria before. But it was rather nice to sit here in New York, talking about my own country to an admirer. Seen in perspective England seemed far less important. To be honest, I'd almost forgotten I lived there. Afterwards, when I told my mother about this episode, she was horrified. 'Fancy going to visit an unknown man at seven-thirty in the morning! You must have been mad. Anything could have happened to you.' 'That will be the day,' I said flippantly. 'Nothing did, unfortunately.' But seriously, I just can't imagine a seduction starting off via Queen Victoria. And who feels like seduction at 7.30 a.m.? John was a very nice man and I'm glad I took the trouble to talk to him.

The American with whom I was lunching just before I left England told me, 'If you want an unforgettable experience, just go down and use our subway system. It's where Dante wrote the *Inferno*.' So I decided, on this last day, to venture down there. I went into the Grand Central Terminal on 42nd Street. What a colossal station: as huge as a cathedral! It took ten years to build and 250,000 passengers use it every day. The ceiling was decorated with what appeared to be groups of stars. On one wall was a clock, twelve feet in diameter, and on another wall the largest photo in the world. So much in America is larger than life. But my American friend was right. Going down into the subway was like entering a pit of foul air and indescribable noise. Our own underground system is no marvel, but it's reasonably clean, as are most of the trains. I came up into the comparatively breathable air as soon as possible. I didn't want that to be my last memory.

I believe that one of the most breath-taking sights of New York is to look out of a high window late at night when the sky is black. The city is one unbelievable mass of illumination, magical and mysterious, a city in the sky. To let your eyes follow the lights down to earth is, with a little imagination, to see brilliant cataracts and waterfalls. I shall always remember New York for that fact alone, and also for its incredible buildings, monuments to the designs of the planners and the skills of workers. Nothing of nature is here, yet it is full of life now, and life about to be.

Back in England, it was easier to describe all this to those who knew nothing, because those who thought they knew the city seemed to me to have no real ideas about it. The men were not all loud-mouthed, cigar-smoking. The women were excellent housewives with spotless homes. The taxi-drivers were not all rude, nor were the public in fear on the streets all the time.

Mr Butterworth told me, 'You'll see, you will like New York far more than Washington. People live here; they only exist there.'

I wonder if he is right?

4: Washington

Driving from New York to the airport we passed a huge and garish sign advertising 'Old Taylor'—whatever that is. Underneath the sign was printed, 'Who are you saving it for!' Of course, this immediately made me think of Albert and how many miles we were apart. Though, as the pace of life up to now had been somewhat energetic, I wasn't sure if there was anything to save. When I told Albert about this, he said, 'Were those the only occasions that you thought about me?' Well, I reckon that he's lucky that I don't think of him as just a roof-provider.

Fortified by drinking a large brandy before boarding the plane, I was less nervous during the take-off. I can't help feeling that the distilling and brewery trade must benefit from people like me who need to consume some of their products before they feel at ease in the air. Well, perhaps not at ease—it's more that one can view possible disaster with detachment.

As we approached Washington, we had a grand view of the Potomac River which, from the air, looked very clean. But on the following day, when I asked a resident in Washington—Henry who is a friend of Toby's—if the Potomac was another polluted river, he replied with a very funny, succinct, and yet also sad remark. 'Anybody can do it. You don't have to be Jesus Christ to walk on this water.'

The drive from the airport through the green countryside was in such contrast to New York, it seemed as though we were in another country, not just another state. There were such beautiful wide avenues, lined with small trees blooming with what I imagined to be a kind of magnolia, but I was told that it was dogwood. It seemed a lovely city, nothing like Boston or New York. Those cities were only a matter of hours away in flying-time, but they were light-years away in atmosphere.

A lot of the houses were built in the old colonial style with stately pillars; others were set back with long gardens in front and looked as though they had cost a fortune.

Some Americans assert that better English is spoken in America than in England. If by this they mean that you can understand them in whatever part of the country you are in, then that statement is true. I could discern no difference in the accents in Washington from those I had heard in Boston and New York. Yet in England I have difficulty in understanding what they are saying in Cornwall or Lancashire; and as for Scotland, although I love the accent, I simply hand over a pencil and paper and ask the speaker to write down what he wants to say. I once had a boy-friend who came from Doncaster and I practically needed an interpreter to understand his conversation. Not that it mattered much, as after a few weeks this consisted of a demand for one thing and my replying with a monosyllable. Naturally, he soon went the way of all boy-friends who find that there's nothing doing.

In spite of the city looking so green and pleasant, like most cities it has problems. I was told that seventy-five per cent of the population are Negroes, and many of them have no work, or prospect of work. When I said to Henry that surely, with such a large percentage of coloured people, some of the plum jobs must have to be given to them, he said that there are no plum jobs—no industry of any kind, which accounted for the city being so clean. The only jobs are in the government and in the university.

One of the very few white taxi-drivers said to me, 'How would you like to live in your capital city if it were nearly all niggers?'

'I thought that you weren't supposed to call them "niggers". In England we say Negroes.'

'Well, you ain't supposed to, but they're still niggers to me and always will be. I'd shoot anybody in my family that I caught with a nigger.'

I wanted to argue with him, but against such intolerance any remark that was the opposite view would have been shouted down. With such a paranoid hatred of black people as he showed, I could never foresee a time coming when black and white would live in harmony in his street.

The section where the Negroes lived was an improvement on the one I had seen in Boston, although Henry said that he wouldn't walk there alone at night.

I was staying at a very attractive and comfortable hotel, the Georgetown Manor on Thomas Jefferson Street. The accommodation was absolutely super, known as the Executive Suite. As well as the bedroom, I had a large sitting-room, and a kitchen, in case I felt like doing a bit of cooking. Actually, I did for a while visualize myself cooking a really superb dinner as a surprise for Toby. But on reflection I decided that he would probably regard it more in the nature of a shock than a surprise; he's not by any means the domesticated type.

In the sitting-room there was a kind of machine in which you inserted a key and turned a knob to select one of a variety of things to eat or drink. Never having seen one of these contraptions, the first time I used it I couldn't find out how to stop it, and some half-dozen cans of Coca-Cola came clanking out. What on earth could I do with all these cans of a beverage that I am not addicted to in its pure form? Now if only there had been a knob to turn to release a bottle of rum, I could have had a celebration all on my own.

Beside the bed there was a kind of box that I took to be a radio until I discovered it was a machine called 'easy sleep'. I tried it out on the first night by putting a coin in the slot. This made the bed vibrate for fifteen minutes, an extremely peculiar sensation. I felt as though I was about to be launched into space any minute. All in all, a poor substitute for Albert—and he has never needed a coin either.

Toby was not staying in the hotel; he was with friends. That man seemed to have friends everywhere, all willing and able to put him up for an indefinite period. With great aplomb he explained to me that the reason he wasn't staying in the hotel was not so that he could remove himself from my company over long periods, but that he was saving money, as the expenses would be less. But I'm not that gullible; I knew he preferred not to face coming down to breakfast. But what about the Gray Line

Tour he had arranged. Was he coming on that? Not on your life. He showed no embarrassment at all when saying, 'Much as I would love to tour the capital of the U.S.A., urgent business on your behalf requires me to forgo that pleasure.' So sincere did he sound that I almost began to believe in his veracity and even to feel sorry for him. I must be getting soft.

Those coach trips really were, on occasions, more in the nature of an endurance test than a pleasurable outing. They dropped you out at various points, and while the driver-guide was taking it easy the passengers embarked on a never-ending walk around. I must admit that the Americans never seemed to flag; they were indefatigable at discovering everything on the tour. As for the cameras, from the smallest box-camera to some so large that I thought they would need to be set up on a tripod, the Americans photographed everything that they were allowed to; and some of the more fanatical practically stood on their heads to get unusual shots. I shuddered to think of how it would be when they got back home. They'd be ringing round all their friends—while they still had them—to come and see the holiday photos. And they'd make sure that you looked at every single one.

One nice feature of a coach trip is that usually the passengers get very neighbourly. In no time at all the people immediately around my seat were all exchanging reminiscences of other trips that they had been on, and when they found that I was from England they started asking me some very awkward questions. They simply couldn't understand that there were places in England that I had never visited. To them it's such a small country that they imagine you can tour it in one day in a car, especially in an American car. I got a bit indignant about this and told them we are a bit bigger than the Isle of Wight. Furthermore, you couldn't possibly get round England in a day. We haven't got freeways and motorways all over the country. In any case, I told them people who live in England just don't want to spend their free time rushing madly from one place to another. They like to sit, to stand and stare, not to have it all planned out.

'Whatever for?' said a gentleman from Nebraska. 'Why, I can get in my car in the morning and drive six hundred miles without a stop-light. I only stop for gas. How would I ever get anywhere if I hadn't made up my mind in advance just where I wanted to go?' There was a general chorus of agreement with this statement, so I kept quiet, much against my inclination as you can be sure. In any case I was practically suffocated as the man next to me was taking up nearly three parts of the seat. No wonder nobody wanted to sit next to him! I had to: it was the only vacant place. I seemed fated to have less than my share of the seat, what with Effie at Boston and now this passenger. My policy of getting on the coach after everybody else was on didn't pay off this time. After four hours together I was almost a grease-spot with the combined heat of the coach and him. He was a very jolly kind of man and each time he laughed he shook so much that, had I been on the outside of the seat, I would have been pushed off. He confided to the bus at large that he weighed sixteen stone and that he intended to go on weighing sixteen stone. He had a wife back in Indiana, who was even heavier; she weighed eighteen stone, which was the reason why she wasn't on this trip.

'Doesn't she ever try to lose some of her weight?' I somewhat cautiously enquired.

'Not likely. I won't let her. I love fat girls; I always have. So I'm not having her change, for who else would love me like she does?'

I couldn't help imagining what sort of love life they had to-gether. The sheer combined weight of them would present some problems as to where, and how, to get amorous. Perhaps they had a specially fortified bed, or had evolved some method of love-making that necessitated very little in the way of sexual gym-nastics. Anyway, I suppose elephants make love.

He showed me a photo of his wife Myrtle and really, consider-ing her size, she looked very attractive. She came from a circus family, and her mother rode a horse bare-backed—the horse, not the mother. I pity any horse that Myrtle tried to sit on. Her father had been an acrobat, and Myrtle was the only one of his six children whom he couldn't train, because she was too fat. Poor Myrtle didn't fit in anywhere. She was too fat to ride a horse and not fat enough to be the fat lady in a side-show. Look-ing at the pictures of Myrtle did wonders for my ego. For if she could be loved, in spite of the mountain of flesh, I needn't worry about the fact that I wasn't exactly sylph-like.

All the American ladies were wearing trouser-suits. I felt some-what out-of-date in wearing a dress, but I have never in my life worn trousers—though a lot of people think I do metaphorically. I did once try a pair on, but I couldn't see that they did anything for me, as I remarked to my sister. She, with devastating can-dour, said there was very little that could—just like my mother who, whenever she sees me in a new hat, never fails to say, 'It looks lovely at the back.'

Our first stop was the Capitol. This splendid building is the American Houses of Parliament. The huge white dome in the centre weighs nine million pounds; on top of it stands a twenty-foot statue of Freedom and, inside, the building has 540 rooms. As hundreds of people were visiting the Capitol, and do so every day, our progress was necessarily slow. I didn't mind this as there was so much to see and hear, especially by the time we reached the Great Hall. The ceiling, 150 feet above, was magnificent, painted with allegorical figures in the inner circle, representing the thirteen original states and the Union, with Washington in the centre between Liberty and Victory. The outer circle symbol-ized the arts, science and commerce. Round the walls were im-mense oil paintings depicting scenes from the Revolution, such as the 'Declaration of Independence' and the 'Surrenders of General Burgoyne and Lord Cornwallis'.

At different periods of American history, four murdered Presi-dents have lain in state in the Great Hall. It's an extremely hazardous undertaking to be an American President, and vulner-able as well. I'm sure people often feel like giving our Prime Ministers a speedy and permanent departure from the cares of office, but nobody goes as far as taking pot-shots at them. Prob-ably we feel that the successor, in spite of all his promises to make England Utopia, will do no better.

We were allowed right into the Senate Chamber to sit in the gallery for ten minutes. There were not many Senators down below and the few that there were appeared not to have the faintest interest in the one who was speaking. This was Senator Tunney from California. He was reading from a paper—always much duller than a speech—about how many dollars America was spending on overseas aid. None of the other Senators even pretended to be listening, but he sure had a rapt audience in the gallery. I felt as though I was in the heart of America, in the middle of great decisions.

So great was the crush of people that we were still proceeding at a snail-like pace. This was the source of great annoyance to a rather belligerent and forceful American, perhaps because he considered that his efforts had helped to put a Senator in the Capitol. 'Goddamn it,' he said, 'what sort of tour is this, standing here for hours, not even allowed to take a picture?' Though I did see him trying to take a picture of the ceiling. He was one of the more pushy types of American that one meets occasionally in England. We all had to listen to his opinions on various subjects whether or not we wanted to hear.

It was somewhat embarrassing for me when we came to the oil-painting representing the 'Declaration of Independence'. 'See that?' said this noisy American. 'That means something, that does. That's when we kicked out the bloody British. We showed them they couldn't run our country. Lot of lousy imperialists they were. As for their king he was as mad as a hatter.'

I kept very quiet while all this ranting was going on. I had no desire to remind him that I was British. Perhaps I ought to have felt patriotic enough to protest at this slight to our royalty. But as I didn't know George III personally, I couldn't see that it was my duty to point out that he wasn't mad all the time; that somebody has discovered he was suffering from porphyria—something to do with the metabolism. However, without consulting me, my large friend nudged the American and said, 'This lady is British.' I could have sunk through the floor. Nevertheless, I thought that the American might have apologized to me for his anti-British remarks. But far from it—all he said was, 'Well, ma'am, we beat you in one war, and helped you to win the last two.' Insufferable man! I suppose, being a stranger in his country, I should not have answered, 'You were a bit late in helping us win the first one.' But I was really irritated by then at his chauvinistic attitude: after all, he wasn't even there. I expected him to be furious at my remark, but surprisingly he burst out laughing, 'Ma'am, you had me there.'

It took us nearly an hour to get round the building, but it was well worth the effort. It really is a beautiful structure, outside and in. I don't wonder the Americans are proud of it.

Our next stop was at the White House. In spite of the fact that Toby was always supposed to be working on my behalf, although I saw precious little evidence of it, he had omitted to inform the President that I was coming; so the President wasn't in residence.

I nearly gave up all thoughts of trying to get in when I saw the length of the queue. From where we were, at the tail-end, you couldn't even see the White House. Simply thousands of people all had the same idea, it seemed. I wonder whether, if Buckingham Palace had conducted tours, crowds would flock to get in. I bet they would. I bet too that the Queen would make sure she wasn't in residence by tripping down to Windsor. I reckon it would be a good way to reduce the national debt. Charge the tourists 25p a time and get them in and out like lightning. People pay to go into these stately homes and nothing could be statelier than Buckingham Palace. They'd have to get rid of those corgis before I'd go, though. I'm not over-fond of dogs, let alone royal ones. Not that I'm keen on visiting these stately homes. One sees only the part that isn't used now. I'd prefer to see how the belted earls live their home-life.

Fifty minutes we stood in that queue before we even reached the gates of the White House. But it wasn't a dull fifty minutes because in the queue was an Australian family, and for me it was marvellous. I was standing there, completely unknown to our group from the bus—except as another sight-seer—when all of a sudden out comes this strong Australian accent, 'You're Margaret Powell; I recognized you from your book. Fancy meeting you here; I must shake your hand.'

Well, I felt like the cat's whiskers, I can tell you, and my stock went up by leaps and bounds. 'Why didn't you tell us you write books?' boomed out Myrtle's husband. 'To think that I sat next to a real author.' Nearly sat on, I thought. Anyway, where would be the point in advertising myself in a country that hasn't yet appreciated how good I am, and doesn't realize what it's missing by not buying my books? But it was something to hear somebody from as far away as Australia saying that they liked them. Once I had a letter from a fan who lived in New Guinea and when I told Albert about it he said, 'I thought that they all wore grass skirts out there.' 'They do,' I told him, 'but they've taught them to read.'

When we finally got inside the White House it was well worth the waiting. Even although I'm British, I felt a kind of pride in walking through these rooms in which every American President except one has lived. It wasn't completed in time for the first President, George Washington.

So great is the queue of people who want to go round the White House that one doesn't have nearly enough time to stand and admire, or to read the copies of famous documents.

It is a beautiful house with fine paintings, lovely china, elegant furniture, and yet not just a house. Even although it was so huge it seemed to emanate the very essence of a home.

Coming away from this place, musing on the many families which had left something of their life and traditions within those walls, I was brought back to reality somewhat abruptly by seeing people lying on the pavement outside. I was told that they were members of the Quaker Peace Corps. All day and all night, year after year, different members had kept vigil there, and would continue to do so until the war in Vietnam was over. Some people were jeering at them, asking what good did they think they were doing by squatting down? What sort of a protest was that? Does it have any effect? I don't know. At least it has been a peaceful protest; that is certainly a change from some that I have read about.

The tour ended with a visit to the Smithsonian Institution. It ended for me as soon as I saw the size of this building. I didn't bother to go in. It was immense, housing a museum of history, technology, fine arts and a portrait gallery. I already felt as though I was training for the Marathon; any further plodding around had had it for me. I was the only one in our bus who ducked out; our driver-guide couldn't understand why. 'It's only another hour,' he told me. 'And there are rest-rooms in the Institution.' Immediately he gave me this information, thoughts of Toby and the lovely rest he was probably having raced furiously through my mind. Whether by rest-rooms he meant the loos I didn't ask. Anyway, it wasn't the loo I needed. Thirty years of living in a house with no indoor sanitation has taught me to suppress the calls of nature. But I would have suppressed it anyway, as it's expensive to use a loo in America. We grumble at having to use a one-pence piece to get in. Here I had to put in a ten-cent piece, worth about eight pence. There was generally one free cubicle without a lock; so if you couldn't reach the door with your foot to keep it shut, it was a bit awkward.

Henry, Toby's friend, has a post at Washington University as a counsellor. Students who have problems bring them to Henry to sort out, and very good he is at doing this, too, judging by his popularity. He is very 'with it' in appearance, with long fair hair and a figure like a lath, and dresses in decrepit-looking jeans. My idea of a counsellor is a wise and venerable old man, long past the adventures of youth, who hasn't forgotten that he once enjoyed them. So I was amazed to learn that Henry, who is about twenty-four and looks even younger, could have this sort of job. Still, I suppose, nowadays wise and venerable old men are about as much wanted by the young as refrigerators in the Arctic.

Henry took Toby and me into the university and we played ten-pin bowling, a game that neither of us had ever played before. I had no idea that the balls were so heavy or that the holes varied in size. I could see that Toby thought playing this game was as easy as falling off a ladder. In fact he was so successful at his first throw that I'm sure he considered himself a champion in the making, even contemplating entering for the Olympics—and standing on that middle step to receive the gold medal. But this flash of brilliance was very soon extinguished. Henry beat both of us, but then he frequently played. Much to my by-no-means-secret gratification, I got a higher score than Toby. Afterwards we sat in the students' recreation room and drank beer until midnight. Henry got some of the students to come over and talk to me, about where they came from and what they hoped to do. It was one of the pleasantest evenings that I had in America.

The following morning, resigned to the absence of Toby at breakfast, I got into conversation with a very talkative American, who introduced himself as Larry.

Because Americans speak English—well it sounds like English —one tends to think that they are exactly like us. Perhaps they were before we lost the country, but, to me, they sometimes seemed just like foreigners who used English words. Needless to say, it was American men that interested me the most. I am long past the age when I expected them to be like the pasteboard heroes of the American films. But I did like most of them. They talked to me as though not only had they all the time in the world to do so but also there was nothing they liked better than conversation with such a charming lady as me. Women count for something here. Perhaps it is my spiritual home—it certainly made me feel about ten years younger. Nevertheless, perhaps it was rather a disappointment not to be able to visualize any one of them as a John Wayne or Clark Gable, who were my favourite heroes. The men I met never seemed to be 'American' so much as Texan, New Yorker or Bostonian. For instance, when Larry heard that I was English and was writing my impressions of America, he said to me, 'You must visit Oklahoma, and Tulsa, where I live.' When I said to him that I thought that was the dustbowl area he sprang to the defence of his state. 'We have the Ozark Mountains and the Arkansas River; it's a thriving community.' So often did I hear this, 'You must come to our state,' or town. When it comes to speaking about the country as a whole, the Americans can be both witty and caustic.

When Larry saw me taking notes he was really concerned to see that I got my facts right. He gave me the titles of various American books that he considered would be a help, in spite of the fact that I told him the book was to be my own impressions, not second-hand words.

'Once this country was made for the poor,' he said, 'now it's made for the take-overs.'

In spite of his flow of non-stop conversation, Larry was, like so many that I met, friendly and welcoming, giving me his home address, to be sure to stay with them if ever I got to Tulsa.

When they come to England I'm sure that they must think of us as somewhat stand-offish.

Larry took me to see the Bureau of Printing and Engraving, where all the American dollars and stamps are made. Not that you can actually be in the very place where it's all turned out on the forever-rolling machines. They don't trust people all that much in America. Or even in Britain come to that: I can't imagine a tour through the Mint with everybody allowed to wander around as they pleased. We all walked through an enclosure and just looked down on all that money being made. What a miser's dream! They print roughly nine million notes every day, using about 1,200 tons of ink and 4,500 tons of paper every year to manufacture this lot. It really was fascinating to see all those stacks and stacks of American dollars. Hopefully I said to Larry, 'Perhaps they will give us a few free samples when we leave.' But needless to say, there was nothing doing. So we had to spend our own money on a meal—or rather, Larry spent his.

He took me to an Italian restaurant, so dark inside that it was like entering a cinema from the sunlight; I had to stand still until Larry led me by the hand to the table. I rather distrust these subterranean places in which it's almost impossible to see just what one is eating. Still, the food was edible and the wine was not so much elegant, as amorous in effect. Good job it was a lunch, and not a dinner. As we were both in such a mellow mood we realized that it would be all wrong to spoil the day by parting company so soon. Where should we go? We decided that, although we were both so intelligent and appreciative of the good things in life, an extra bit of culture wouldn't do us any harm. So why not a visit to the National Gallery of Art, one of America's most important galleries? It's a very attractive building; another of America's largest; in this case the 'largest marble structure in the world'—rose-white Tennessee marble. There is a superb collection of Italian paintings and two entire rooms devoted to Rembrandt. I'm not like some experts, who say that no matter how many times they view a particular painting, they see each time something in it that they never noticed before—a new perspective, a fresh idea of the painter's art. All I can say is, they're lucky. Each new gallery I go in, the pictures look just the same as in the preceding one; I can't pretend that I see anything except what's visible to everybody. What I did enjoy looking at were the American paintings of the colonial days. There were very few people viewing these; don't they value their own artists?

Larry was leaving Washington late that afternoon, so we parted with many expressions of mutual regret at having to say goodbye. I went back to the hotel, and to pass the time while I was waiting to hear from Toby, who as usual was nowhere to be seen or contacted, I wandered around Georgetown. This is a very attractive part of Washington. Once it was a very busy colonial town and seaport. There are still many old houses in the colonial style of architecture with red cobbled pavements and spacious gardens. In 1950 Congress approved an act relating to Georgetown, 'to preserve and protect the places and areas of popular interest'. Would that our Parliament would pass such a law about London before the city is finally given over to the developers!

I took a taxi to the Lincoln Memorial, which has the largest statue I have ever seen—of President Lincoln. At night when it's illuminated it's really something—though Henry made some very caustic remarks about what was the good of it. I did have ideas of going to the top of the Washington Monument, all 555 feet of it, but decided that heroism could be carried too far.

In the taxi, going back to the Georgetown Manor, I couldn't help looking at the driver's nose; it was squashed as flat as a pancake. Unfortunately, he saw me looking, so I asked him if he had been in an accident.

'Well, I suppose you could call it that. It sure wasn't intentional when my nose met a fist as hard as iron.'

Mr Ellis had been a boxer, and a good one too, he said. He'd won lots of important fights. But owing to the lack of a good manager to negotiate the fees, he had never got half the money he should have had. I sympathized with him over this. Mr Ellis spoke very nostalgically of London, although he had never been there. 'Life is quieter there,' he said, 'people have time to stop and be neighbourly.' I forbore to tell him that I hadn't noticed very much of the good-neighbour policy in London. Why should I destroy a person's illusions?

It transpired that he got this information from two aunts of his who lived 'just outside London'.

'Whereabouts outside?' I asked, thinking that he meant one of the suburbs.

'Luton.'

Well, I suppose if you are living in such a vast country as America, Luton does seem to be 'just outside London'. Probably to an American, even the Isle of Wight is just outside London.

It was late evening before Toby managed to find time from his arduous life to come round to the hotel. But at least he had arranged what we were doing on the following day. Henry was driving us to the Shenandoah Valley.

I reckon that this was the very best day, when Henry took us in his car to this lovely place, over a hundred miles from Washington. I couldn't believe at first that he was prepared to give up so much of his time for our pleasure, but he was, and he did. Toby really does have some charming friends; perhaps there is more to him than I know of. He insisted that we should first drive to the Arlington National Cemetery to see the Kennedy graves. It is beautifully kept, with row after row of simple small white headstones marking the graves of the American soldiers killed in battle. Three Unknown Soldiers are buried there from the First and Second World Wars and the Korean War. Crowds of people continuously go there to view the Kennedy graves. I think it is right that all these people continually come to honour the American dead, and be reminded of what war really means.

On the way to the Shenandoah Valley we drove through mile after mile of country—little villages, green trees and clean roads. This last could be accounted for by the signs at regular intervals, which stated, 'Drivers subject to arrest for throwing litter from vehicles'. 'Arrest', I noted, not a fine. In all those miles of roads that we drove along, there were no bottles or tin cans, old mattresses or rusty bike-frames. Some of the cities might look as though all the rubbish were thrown from the windows to the cries of 'gardyloo'—or the American equivalent—but not the countryside. Pity we are not harsher on rubbish-leavers. Some of our country roads give the appearance of national junkyards.

We stopped at a Hamilton Inn—this is like a super Wimpey. I was persuaded to try root-beer as a change from cola. Awful stuff! God knows what they make it from; it is nothing like real beer.

Driving along the high road we could see, far below, the Shenandoah River. I had no idea that the river was in America. The name sounds sort of Persian, though actually it's a tributary of the Potomac. My mother used always to be singing the sea-shanty 'Oh Shenandoah, I long to see you, roll away you rolling river'. Why she sang this I have no idea, especially as she disliked the water and her only experience of being on it was a trip from Brighton Palace Pier to Portsmouth. She was so violently sea-sick that she made the return journey by train, telling my father that he could go back on his own on the boat. For my mother to let Dad loose among trippers without her just shows how her resistance had been weakened.

The Shenandoah National Park is a wonderful place, three hundred square miles of it, full of valleys and hollows, refreshing little streams and sparkling waterfalls; masses of shrubs, wild flowers—which nobody is allowed to pick—shady paths, and birds continually flying in and out of the great profusion of trees. One would need weeks of leisure to explore the half of it. In the distance, I could see mile after mile of the Blue Ridge Mountains, bluey-grey, ridge following ridge, other worldly, like some lunar landscape. It belongs to the Tertiary Period when the only signs of life were the molluscs, and little imagination was needed to visualize a time when from the vast rocks crawled dinosaurs and other prehistoric animals. Some of these rock formations had names like Hogback Wallow, Rattlesnake Point and Brokenback Mountain.

Henry tried to alarm me by saying that ferocious bears still roamed the park and were liable to attack any visitor; but as there were no warning notices up about this, I didn't believe it. Besides, I don't think that bears are ferocious animals unless they are starving.

One rather sad sight was the number of trees that have perished from the ravages of a species of caterpillar. These encase their larvae in a ball like an orange, sometimes even larger; then they spin white triangular ghost-like webs across the branches. It looks for all the world like something out of science fiction. When the larvae break out of their ball, they eat away at the bark of tree after tree until each tree dies. Short of felling thousands of trees, and that is not practical, there is nothing as yet known to stop the ravages of these insects.

On the way back from Shenandoah we stopped at a wayside farm where they had home-made cider for sale; we drank a glass, which was deliciously fresh and cold. Henry bought a couple of bottles and then invited Toby and me to a meal to help drink it. I went into a giant supermarket with him to buy some food. This one was by no means the largest of the supermarkets, but by our standards it was colossal. It was also one of the most clinical and impersonal places that I have shopped in. Not an assistant was to

69

be seen; in these vast establishments the manufacturers have their allotted shelves and keep them replenished. So huge is the place that one hardly has any contact with the other customers. It was the silence that I noticed above all.

Henry decided to barbecue steak for our meal. I had never seen this done, or eaten meat cooked in this way. It certainly made a lot of smoke. Unless one had a very large garden I couldn't see it being done outdoors in England. Some irate neighbour would very soon be knocking on one's door to complain that the smoke was ruining her washing, or the windows had just been cleaned. I'll admit that the steak tasted delicious, but I reckon that was because the meat was good, rather than that Henry was a skilful cook. Personally, I don't go for this fetish of eating out of doors. I prefer to eat in civilized surroundings with all the proper accessories. Maybe my phobia against the outdoor life dates back to the occasion when I went out picnicking with a new boy-friend who I hoped—in vain—would become a permanent attachment. It was I who had suggested this picnic and had made various dainties such as vol-au-vents and sausage rolls. We strolled through some fields on this really idyllic day and I felt as though I was in heaven, even though all the conversation consisted of my agreeing with everything that he said. One had to make sacrifices in those days. I remember that he talked all the time mostly about all the places he had visited, and all the out-of-the-ordinary things he had done. After an hour or two we decided to eat. I laid the cloth on the grass, set out everything, chose what appeared to be a nice patch of grass and sat on a wasp. It gave me a ferocious sting and the pain was intense. Of all the embarrassing places to be stung! I couldn't even show it to the young man—well, one couldn't, and didn't, in those days.

After the meal was over and I was sitting in Henry's room, feeling that all was for the best in the best of all possible worlds, I was abruptly brought back to reality by Toby. He said that it was time to drive back to the hotel as he and Henry had an engagement for the evening.

I was so choked with rage at being thus discarded without so much as a 'do you mind' that I simply couldn't speak. The very idea of us all spending the day and half the evening together, and then to be casually dropped off like an unwanted spare part! It wasn't that I was longing to go with them: I wasn't, because in point of fact I had, unbeknown to Toby, arranged to go out with one of the residents of the hotel. No, what riled me was Toby's calm assumption that ten o'clock was the end of the day for me. I don't know why I hadn't liked to tell him about my evening arrangement. After all, I was a free agent and he wasn't supposed to be looking after my moral welfare. He knew that I could take care of myself, unlike Michael, who took over later on and who, much to my astonishment and sometimes fury, practically constituted himself my jailer. Because I still didn't feel that I knew Toby, it often seemed to me that he was sitting in judgment on things that I said and did. Probably because he was not talkative, I tended to feel that he would not bother with trivial conversation, when the truth could have been that he had nothing to say, like Albert, my husband, who can sit in a chair, silent, and gaze at nothing for hours. I used to think that he sat and thought great thoughts, but later on I realized that he just sat.

Paul, the man who was taking me out, was a German, a positive bean-pole of a man. Most Americans seemed to be overweight. He informed me in the first five minutes that he had a wife and four children back in Frankfurt—that was fine by me. I justified going out with him because I had to have material for the book. He had a huge car but was a maniacal driver, tearing along as though demons were pursuing us. We went some miles from the hotel, and although I had so recently eaten, I agreed when he suggested stopping to eat. I was so relieved to find I was still alive after that car ride that I would have agreed to anything. We had Frankfurter sausages which, so Paul said, were made in exactly the way they make them in his native city, with coriander seeds, claret, pork, all put into sausage skins and boiled in beer. They were very good served with apple sauce.

The whole time we were together Paul was moaning about the deficiencies of the British workman. He owned a factory in Frankfurt that made electrical equipment of some kind, and had got thirty British from England to work in his factory. Of the original thirty, only five now remained. The others had gone back to England, disgruntled at the long hours with no tea-breaks and only a half-hour midday meal.

'Don't talk to me about British workmen,' said Paul. 'They

don't want to work; they're soft. What do they expect for the equivalent of sixty pounds per week? An eight-hour day and two hours out of that to loll around smoking?' Well, one would need to know just how far the money went in Germany for food and lodging to know whether sixty pounds was a good wage or not.

But honestly, I began to think that it was a mistake to leave England if one wanted to feel that people liked us. What with listening to the American version of the War of Independence, and this German version of the demerits of the British worker, was anybody ever going to praise our country? Perhaps it was because in Washington, with its Capitol that the British burned and smashed, we were not much liked. All would be different in New Orleans.

As usual, I was very glad and relieved to see Toby on the morning of our departure. I don't know where he went overnight but it really was funny to see him. He had a terrific hangover and looked like nothing on earth—and not at all heavenly.

I had come to no harm, and was feeling on top of the world, which fact I hastened to tell Toby at the earliest opportunity. I cannot say with truth that he received this news with any satisfaction—rather the reverse, in fact.

We were leaving from Dallas Airport, miles away from Washington. Henry was driving us there. We drove through miles of country, with not a habitation in sight. Suddenly, out of nowhere it seemed, this huge airport loomed up. Henry, always a mine of information, told us that the reason the airport was built in this wilderness was that within the next fifteen years Washington would extend nearly as far. Toby, sunk in gloom, muttered that as far as he was concerned, there was enough of Washington already; any more could be consigned to perdition.

5 : New Orleans

At Dallas Airport, while waiting for the plane to New Orleans, I went into the café, very clean and clinical. I ordered coffee, as America's idea of tea-making results in an undrinkable concoction. All the other customers seemed to be eating doughnuts, first dunking them in their coffee, so I thought that I would try one. But I didn't like it at all. Goodness knows what they use to make them—maize flour, perhaps. The waitress got into conversation by saying, 'Bet you don't get doughnuts like that in England. Nobody can make waffles, pancakes and doughnuts like we can.' As far as I was concerned she never spoke a truer word.

At the time I didn't realize that this was just the first of a chain of mishaps, forming a somewhat unpleasant introduction to New Orleans. For it was not a pleasant journey on the plane. We went through a thunderstorm; the sky was absolutely black. The absence of anything to eat added to the discomfort—eating does soothe my nerves. I said that they couldn't serve food because of the turbulence, but Toby insisted it was because there wasn't time. He assured me that the absence of food wasn't a great loss, as on these internal flights it generally consisted of hamburgers or great wedges of sandwiches.

As the sky got darker and darker, I became almost petrified with fright and thought that any minute the plane would be struck by lightning. I had never flown through a thunderstorm before. My fears were not allayed by Toby's boast that he had been in far worse storms, where he was literally thrown about in the plane. I have never found that the sufferings of other people alleviate one's own, and as usual Toby's conversation was limited to an occasional, 'Are you all right?' I don't know what he contemplated doing in the event of my saying, 'Far from it.' I was in need of a lot of sympathy, not just a few laconic enquiries.

Then it was raining when we landed at New Orleans. In the taxi from the airport the driver said that it had rained non-stop for four days and nights.

We were booked at an enormous hotel with three swimming pools, though the third one must have been designed for midgets. That's about all this hotel did have to recommend it, and I am not much of a swimmer. What was required was less ostentation and better service. When we tried to book in we might not have existed for all the notice the staff took. After I had practically defied death to get here, I certainly expected, if not a hero's welcome, somebody to notice that I had arrived.

We went downtown afterwards and the streets were absolutely deserted and quiet. I asked the taxi-driver if it was always like that on a Sunday evening. He said that it was too dangerous to walk in the streets late at night, and that he wasn't too keen on going through them in his taxi, even, as within the last two months two drivers had been murdered.

'I carry a gun,' he said to us, 'and at night I take only one man for a fare. I say to him, you sit in the front seat with me, and you keep your hands on your lap where I can see them, or else I might blow them right off.'

What a charming driver, and what a pleasant way to have a taxi-ride! Had I defied death in the clouds only to meet it at the hands of a trigger-happy cab-man? I thought with some nostalgia of London taxis, where one doesn't sit behind a bullet-proof screen looking at a driver with his gun.

Toby and I had already decided to move from this hotel, so we asked the taxi-driver if he knew of a decent one in the French Quarter.

'This hotel we are in now doesn't seem to know, or care, if you are dead or alive,' we told him. 'Why should they care? You're in America now, not in England,' was all the help we got.

We were fortified in the decision to move when we had breakfast the following morning. Mine arrived about forty-five minutes later than I had ordered it, and was awful; the toast I should imagine had made the rounds of several bedrooms before ending up with me. The soft-boiled egg was so hard that it literally bounced when I dropped it on the floor.

But fortunately this was the end of our troubles, for we managed to book in at the Sonesta Hotel, right in the French Quarter. This hotel had a friendlier atmosphere and I felt much happier, even though the air-conditioning in my bedroom made a noise reminiscent of a steam-roller ploughing its way up and down the street.

Now that we were settled I was looking forward to seeing a lot of New Orleans, having been told that it was a fascinating city. To save Toby making excuses about being busy I didn't wait for him to suggest a tour but actually offered to arrange it for myself. So my astonishment was great when Toby told me that the tour was already settled, and that he was coming with me. I certainly never expected that he would make such a sacrifice.

In the event, it was the quickest conducted tour that I have ever made. The driver was a non-stop talker, and kept up a flow of facetious remarks about other trips he had done. I could see that Toby was becoming incensed by this increasing babble. Any minute I expected him to stand up in the coach and call out, 'Stop the coach! I want to get off.'

The first stop that the driver made was at an arty shop, called 'Trash and Treasure'. They must have hidden the treasure because all that we could see was trash. Then we went through a dingy little courtyard at the back, which the driver assured us was the oldest in New Orleans; by the look of it I could well believe him. Toby said that he knew of several far better ones; and he was right; he did. He and I did our own personal tour from this point, and abandoned the driver and his coach. I was glad that Toby had so abruptly terminated our tour. As we wandered through street after street on our own, the charm and fascination of New Orleans seemed to create a kind of harmony, as though we were not strangers to the city. I know that I felt welcomed as I slowly walked through this old French Quarter which is much the same as it was in the eighteenth century.

Although Toby showed not the slightest sign of guilt at discarding the coach and the tour—he didn't even mention to the driver that we were leaving—I did feel somewhat embarrassed, even more so when, later on in the day, we were sitting on two low posts in a narrow street and the bus came through at a snail's pace. Everybody gazed at us; I know that they considered us as deserters.

The modern world seemed very remote among these lovely old houses, very straight and narrow streets, and dozens of beautiful cool, green and shady little patios. Toby took me into one that had a fountain in the middle and beautiful iron railings that looked like lace. I drank mint julep, which I'd never tasted before in my life. It's made with just Bourbon whiskey, crushed ice and mint, and I found it very potent. Of course, the surroundings could have contributed to this effect. Sitting in a shady courtyard listening to the tinkling of the fountain had already induced a state of bliss. I'm sure that a mint julep drunk in a British railway buffet wouldn't taste the same at all. As it's very hot in New Orleans all the bars and courtyards are windowless and dark; this is very pleasant after the bright sunshine.

As we continued walking we came across more attractive old houses where it seemed that time had stood still, so well preserved were they.

One of the most thrilling moments that I had was to stand by the Mississippi River. There was a boat going down the river, right out of *Showboat*. Any minute I expected to hear a great bass voice rolling out 'Old Man River'. In fact I nearly started singing myself, I was so overcome at seeing this great river. I can on occasions get sentimental. Only out of consideration for Toby, who had on this trip been a very enjoyable companion, did I refrain from bursting into song as we walked back to the hotel.

This hotel was really an improvement on the other; my breakfast arrived punctually to the minute. When I ordered it over the telephone, I tentatively enquired whether I could have tea in a teapot.

'You certainly can,' a very pleasant voice replied, 'and you can have an extra tea-bag.' I immediately had visions of a lovely pot of strong tea. But when it arrived, oh dear! The teapot turned out to be a glass carafe of hot water into which I had to drop two tea-bags. By the time the breakfast reached me the water was a long way off the boil.

As Toby had a friend that he wanted to meet—even here he

had friends—I wandered down into the French Quarter again. Outside one of the antique shops was sitting an old man. He was carving the most intricate shapes in wood, using just a pocket-knife. He reminded me of a sailor I used to know who was good at whittling; unfortunately that was about the only thing that he was any good at—as far as I was concerned, anyway. If he had any other powers he never demonstrated them in my direction; not for the want of encouragement either. This Jimmy was for ever making me useless little animals that I hadn't a clue what to do with, as I was in domestic service and had nowhere to put them. I never have been a collector. It's too much bother looking after the objects. Jimmy was the second young man I had who was clever with his hands. The first one, after a few weeks, got too clever. The quickness of the hand may deceive the eye, but his moves didn't deceive me.

I just couldn't leave off gazing at the old houses set in avenues of trees. There was a particularly beautiful house with wrought-iron balconies all round, which was built in 1838. In another one lives the novelist, Frances Parkinson Keyes. Yet another old house had a fascinating iron fence with a cornstalk design and pumpkins at the base. Gazing at this, oblivious of passers-by, I was nearly knocked down by a man—and what a man! Well over six feet tall. In an enchanting American voice he apologized most profusely, though it really wasn't his fault. He insisted on buying me a drink. Well, he didn't have to insist all that much as I was dying to try another mint julep. His home was in Dallas, Texas, but, he said, 'I'm neither a cattle baron nor an oil millionaire. Just an ordinary American travelling on business, and feeling a bit lonely.' We got on like a house on fire; that lovely voice really got me. Strangely enough, he liked my accent, which he presumed was Cockney. He had been in England only once, but hoped to visit it again next year. I invited him to my home. I wonder if he will seem so attractive divorced from his natural surroundings. I arranged to meet him early on the following day, though I didn't know quite how I was going to manage this, as Toby had booked us breakfast at Brennan's; you couldn't get in without booking. 'Breakfast at Brennan's'! I'm sure it beats breakfast at Tiffany's. It was out of this world. Such a breakfast at nine o'clock in the morning! We started with oyster soup, and milk punch, which I had never tasted before. It was delicious, so we had another one while we waited for the wine that Toby had ordered. When it did arrive Toby had the nerve to send it back. He said it wasn't cold enough. Fancy having the nerve to send back wine at that hour of the morning! Sometimes I think Toby doesn't live in the real world, but in one of his own invention. Then we had Eggs Hussarde, which is grilled ham on toast covered with a wine sauce. This is topped with poached eggs and hollandaise sauce and served with grilled tomatoes. I ate the lot, though Toby couldn't manage his. Then I finished up with bananas sautéd in rum, butter and brown sugar and served on ice cream. Toby had a crêpe suzette.

We had dined at Antoine's the previous evening and that was an experience. I kept saying to myself, 'Dinner at Antoine's! Talk about living!' But 'Breakfast at Brennan's' is even better. It is redolent of gracious living. Lovely patios, rustling palms, fine food and impeccable service; everything harmonizes. It was a once-in-a-life-time meal. Afterwards, Toby had to retire to rest— he lacks stamina—so I was able to go to meet Lee. We went around admiring the Creole architecture and browsing in the antique shops. Lee bought me an old brooch; at least the proprietor said that it was old, but I have my doubts. However, one doesn't look a gift horse in the mouth. Lee said that he had heard of a place where hectic real old jazz was played; not everybody could get in but he could get both of us in. The only drawback was that it didn't start until midnight, but we could visit two famous jazz halls earlier in the evening: Preservation Hall and Heritage Hall.

Lee was staying in a hotel on the same street as ours, Bourbon Street. I arranged to meet him in the foyer of our hotel soon after ten o'clock. Toby had arranged to take me around New Orleans in the evening to see a bit of night-life, and there was plenty of it: crowds of people, dressed in all the colours of the rainbow, and music seemed to come from every doorway. We went into Pat O'Brien's to eat. This place, the building and courtyard, was built in 1792 as the first Spanish theatre in the United States. It is now a very pleasant place indeed to be in, to wine and dine. There are pianists, and any member of the audience who thinks that he can sing, is very welcome to do so. Needless to say, out of consideration for Toby, I didn't.

I began to get inwardly agitated as to how I could get back to the hotel in time for Lee. What excuse could I make? Finally, in desperation I told a very surprised Toby that I was tired and would like to have an early night.

'Tired? You're never tired. Why, it's not ten o'clock yet.' Still he didn't take much persuading; he likes a lot of rest himself. By the time that we got back to the hotel I had only just enough time to have a shower before meeting Lee downstairs. One needed to keep on having showers because, even in early May, it was very hot and sticky. Everywhere was air-conditioned—hotels, buses, shops. Some of the large departmental stores had the air-conditioning just outside the entrance and shoppers stood underneath it to chat. It's really quite odd to take one step into the cool shop, and then one step out into intense heat. It's a very humid heat and although I was enjoying this city, I wasn't sorry to know that I would be gone before the temperature reached 90°, as it does later on in the year.

I felt somewhat guilty that I had not told Toby I was going out again. I suppose I ought to have done; but I didn't want an inquest. 'Who is he? Where is he staying and where are you going?' To none of these questions could I have given satisfactory answers. Besides, I was afraid that Toby might have decided to come with us. That would have been hopeless. For not only was I certain that Lee wouldn't expect to see Toby as well as me; I also knew that they would not get on well together as Lee had a very extrovert nature; he laughed at his own jokes. In any case, I felt that I was justified in what I was doing. It was solely to get material for the book, not for my pleasure only. And for all I could prove to the contrary, Toby went out every night after I was safely in my room. Just because he came upstairs at the same time as I did didn't mean that he stayed there. I just could not believe that somebody as young as Toby never went to bed later than midnight, when night-life was going on to 4 a.m.

Anyway that's my justification—that I was doing it for the book. After all, you can't write about your impressions if you never go anywhere to get them. I met Lee downstairs and rushed him out of the hotel like lightning, in case I was seen. He took me into a bar and bought me an absinthe; at least that's what he said it was. I had never drunk it before in my life. What a ghastly drink! The dictionary says that absinthe is an extract of worm-wood. I can well believe it—and that it's mixed with raw alcohol. It is supposed to induce a feeling of euphoria and you cease to want to drink at all—because you have ceased to breathe, I reckon. Nothing would have induced me to drink a second one, not while I was out at midnight with a stranger, anyway. I had not forgotten the tequila.

We went first to Preservation Hall, where the real, true old jazz was being played. The hall is a house, about a hundred and fifty years old, which has never been altered or done up. By the look of it, it had never been redecorated either. There are abso-lutely no concessions made to comfort. It's a dirty old room, with bare wooden floor, and just hard backless benches to sit on. Yet every night it is packed with jazz devotees. And it was marvel-lous jazz, played by about six performers, all getting on in years —clarinet, trombone, drums, piano and banjo. The heat was in-tense, and we had to stand at the back, but I felt no discomfort; I could have listened for hours, there was such a feeling of pleasure in listening to this interpretation of jazz as it should be. Or so I thought.

As there was still time to kill before midnight, Lee and I went into the other jazz hall, Heritage. Here also real traditional jazz was played. If possible, this was even better than Preservation, so exciting to listen to that I wanted to stamp with the beat. It re-minded me of the jazz that I used to hear years ago when I went dancing. The players, who were obviously enjoying themselves, were all elderly. It does seem sad to realize that when these have gone their kind of music will be found only on records. I bought one as a memento.

We stayed there until Lee reminded me that it was twelve o'clock, time to leave. After walking through several dark and narrow streets we arrived at a very old-looking house; Lee passed over money and we went down into what was little more than a cellar, lit by unshaded electric bulbs. It had bare walls; it was scruffy in the extreme and stinking hot. It seemed to be crowded with people, mostly white. At one end of the room were three very dark men, wearing nothing but red satin trousers. Rivulets of sweat were running down their bare bodies. One was banging on a pair of bongo-drums; one had what looked like a trumpet but a bit different; the other had cymbals and other instruments. At first I was disappointed, because you couldn't call it jazz. But after an hour or two, what with the heat, crowd and the odd drink, that music really got you. It went stamp, stamp, and then would come a sound that reminded you of voodoo and fertility rites in the African jungle. In a way it was frightening because it was so uninhibited. Towards the end some of the audience were dancing round and round in a ring and the women were taking off their dresses and prancing round in their bras and panties. I didn't remove any of my clothes; not likely. I never did go in for this audience participation, and I much preferred the real jazz, such as we had heard earlier, where audience participation just consisted of laughing and stamping of the feet, and everybody looked happy. 'Happy' wasn't the word for how they looked here; it was more as though they were mesmerized.

By now I'd had enough and wanted to leave but I could see by the glazed expression in Lee's eyes that he really thought, 'This is life with a capital L.' He said to me, 'This is what people are really like. Civilization and the wearing of conventional clothes are just a veneer.' Well, it was a veneer that I wasn't going to crack—not likely! If this was real life, all these adults stamping around half undressed—and most of them looked much better with their clothes on—then give me the artificial. You do know the rules. Besides, the primitive life is all right so long as it's thousands of miles away. I couldn't imagine Lee giving up his air-conditioned, centrally-heated house in Dallas, or his two cars, to go back and live with nature.

I finally persuaded him to take me back at 3 a.m. I was half asleep, but Lee was so stimulated that any minute I thought he would leap into the trees and emulate Tarzan calling for his mate. Thank heaven that wouldn't have been me. Big and strong as he was, Lee could hardly have swung from tree to tree carrying me.

We parted in the foyer of my hotel, where, as there were still people milling around, Lee could not envelop me in a bear-like embrace.

'We must do it again another evening,' he said enthusiastically.

'Certainly, we will,' I said aloud, inwardly saying to myself, 'Not on your life we won't; enough's enough.'

As I went past Toby's room I resisted the temptation to bang on it.

What enormous newspapers these Americans have! Surely they can't possibly read all of them? When I bought the *New York Times* I thought I had picked up several newspapers by mistake, there was such bulk. Perhaps New Yorkers know how to read it; I couldn't find any news that I wanted. There were masses of advertisements for about everything under the sun, and the most nondescript news about uninteresting places and people, surely more suitable for a local paper. But the paper this morning, 8 May, was full of the news that President Nixon would continue the bombing of North Vietnamese lines of supply and also would lay mines in the Port of Haiphong. Later on in the morning when I was having a coffee I got talking to an American family from New York. The son was about twenty and the daughter twenty-five. The young man spoke very bitterly of President Nixon. 'Why doesn't he pull out? He's clever enough to make it appear that we have won the war, even although we have lost it.' He reckoned that Nixon had ruined his chances of being re-elected. The parents thought that Nixon was doing the best he could in a very difficult situation.

Later on, I watched the news on television. Twelve ordinary people, who had been approached on their way to work, were in the television studio to give their views on the situation. Like most people who are suddenly asked to talk on an important subject, they were somewhat confused. They were all asked for their opinion. Should Nixon let the war go on and bomb the supply lines? Should he pull out or was it right that he should blockade the port and stop the supplies, that came mainly from Russia? One young man gave his opinion very forcefully, 'It's all wrong. How can you bomb supply lines and not kill innocent civilians?' Another man said that to blockade the port now was far too late; it should have been done years ago. A very inarticulate elderly woman kept on repeating, 'I try to think what I would have done in the same circumstances; I really don't know.' Not much help to the interviewer! The most lucid was a man who said that the President was all wrong to think that the North Vietnamese would negotiate. Why should they? They were doing all right in the war. He reckoned that Nixon could well have tolled the bell to start the next World War. He was also sure, and, as it turned out, he was right, that students would be staging violent anti-war demonstrations all over the country as soon as they had finished sitting through their finals. The interview ended, as far as I could tell, with about six against Nixon, five 'don't knows' and the elderly woman still saying, 'What would I have done? I really don't know,' as the interviewer ushered her off the screen.

I have never seen anything like American television. It seems to be on for twenty-two hours out of the twenty-four. One hears many adverse comments regarding its quality, but I think the marvel is that with so many hours of viewing time, it's as good as it is. A lot of the time is used up showing old films that weren't much good when they were new, and have not improved in any way over the years. There are chat shows galore, with the interviewers full of bonhomie and an endless fund of jokes. But above all there are the commercials. Colourful, often witty and amusing, they permeate the entire life of American television. It seemed to me that every film or play that I watched was broken into at intervals of five minutes by some advertisement. I was exhorted by beautiful young ladies to buy this soap, or that perfume, or face-cream. Are you afraid that 'Your best friends won't tell you'? Then buy this toothpaste or deodorant. For every ailment under the sun there was a remedy, often portrayed by the most lurid diagrams of your digestive system. In fact, I believe that I have learnt more about my anatomy from American television than from any other source.

Our stay in New Orleans was nearly over, but there were still some interesting places I had not yet seen. I was sitting in my room wondering whether I should go on a coach tour when the telephone rang. It was my Texan friend suggesting just that. I knew that Toby would not really want to come even if he agreed to it just to please me. He spent most of each day in, or by, the swimming pool. He does seem to require a great deal of rest. Goodness knows why, unless he leads a riotous life at night. I wasn't too keen on going with Lee because he had a habit of comparing everything in New Orleans with Texas. According to Lee, Texas had everything in the way of scenery, climate, buildings and wonderful people.

This tour took in a lot of historical points, such as Jackson Square. This was given its name in honour of General Andrew Jackson when he defeated the British at the Battle of New Orleans. I began to wonder whether our driver was a descendant of General Jackson, for he certainly went to great length and detail to tell us how heroic was the General's defence against the rampaging and licentious British soldiers. The soldiers had looted the town and raped the women. Why is it, I wonder, that soldiers are always accused of raping after a battle? I would have thought that they were too tired. Perhaps the excitement releases a lot of adrenalin—is it adrenalin that's needed? Years later, the citizens of New Orleans met to nominate Andrew Jackson for President. The Americans on the bus expressed their pride in all this glorious past. They really do seem to have far more national pride than we do.

Lee asked me what I thought about it. I didn't like to say that I, and most of England, couldn't care less about losing America —that if people in England think about it at all, they think that we were well shot of it. Fortunately, I was saved the embarrassment of having to give a diplomatic reply. The driver stopped the coach and we all got off to view St Louis Cathedral, the oldest cathedral in the nation, our driver said. This one dates from 1794 but there were two earlier ones on the same site. We walked along Pirates' Alley through which pirates were taken, chained together, to jail.

The coach went along by the Mississippi, and Lee started rhapsodizing about this river, about how many states it flowed through, and how, with the Missouri, it was the longest river in the world. I hastily interrupted to let him know that I had learnt all that information in school. He wanted to take me on the Mississippi river-boat. I would have loved that, to be able to say that I really had been *on* the Mississippi. Unfortunately we were too late; the boat had gone. Still, he did try, which was more than anybody else had done.

That Lee was a charming man. Because he knew that I was writing about America, and wanted to talk to Americans, he got into conversation with a couple in the seat in front of us. They were from New York, a Mr and Mrs Watson. Mr Watson was a teacher and they had lived in England for a year on one of the exchange visits. Mrs Watson had liked England, and even, after a while, English people, although she just could never forget the English winter. It wasn't that it was colder than in America, but the fact that nothing was done to make the winter endurable. She was very funny about our failings. Surely our houses were the draughtiest places to live in! Never a door but the wind blew through the bottom of it! We had no idea of double glazing, or storm porches; as for the plumbing, absolutely archaic! What on earth made builders put the pipes outside the house so that in the first frost they froze up and eventually burst? And why was the coal-bunker always out in the open, so that every time you wanted coal you got soaked in the rain, slipped over in the snow or lost your way in the dark? And the fireplace, set so far in that you had to crouch like a hunchback to get warm! She hadn't, of course, expected to find central heating or air-conditioning; nevertheless she had expected some of the benefits of an advanced technology. Why, we had hardly any kitchen gadgets!

By this time poor Lee began to wish he had never started the conversation; he didn't want me to get upset at this denigration of the English way of life. In fact, it made me laugh, but at the same time I was inwardly marshalling my arguments against what I had decided to call the gadget-ridden and artificial way of American life.

'We like being what you call "primitive",' I told her. 'It makes life anything but dull. It's quite an adventure when one opens a can with an ordinary tin-opener and manages to do it without inflicting a fatal wound.' Warming up to the subject, I added, 'As for the plumbing, how would plumbers live when they were not installing pipes in new houses, if nobody needed their services for burst pipes? Why, we keep them off the dole. Besides, look how it passes the time. Several hours can be spent on a bitterly cold morning in telephoning round trying to get someone to stop your leaking pipes and unstop your frozen loo.'

Carrying on the attack I went on, 'What about your letter-boxes? If I am carrying parcels and I want to post a letter, I've got to put some of the parcels down because I need two hands, one to pull down the handle and the other to post the letter. Why can't you have proper pillar-boxes like ours? Furthermore, one is never sure what clothes cost because the tax is added on afterwards. Why can't it be inclusive like our purchase tax? And how awkward your money is! Why do you make ten cents a smaller coin than five cents? No wonder I get muddled when it comes to tipping. And talking about tipping, your system is even more iniquitous than ours; it seems to be necessary to tip everybody to get any kind of service.'

By this time we decided that honours were even, and as it was time for refreshment we all four sat down for coffee. We were joined by another American family from the bus—parents with three children, aged from six to thirteen.

Much has been written about American children, mostly to their detriment. How ill-mannered, demanding and blasé they are. These children were charming, in no way shy or gawky. Sometimes I think that the American child has it made from the start—the well-to-do one, anyway. He seems to be treated as an adult from the earliest age. He eats with the grown-ups, at home and in restaurants; he is encouraged to give an opinion on any subject. He seems not to have the shyness, the inability to communicate of the English child. He may be behind English children academically, but he is certainly ahead socially.

The four of us went shopping for souvenirs in a place called Brulatour Courtyard. This is lined with delightful little shops, full of worthwhile souvenirs and antiques. What I liked particularly was that one could browse around without finding an assistant hovering near, or being asked, 'Can I help you?' Mr Watson bought a lovely amber necklace for his wife; I really coveted it. With a little persuasion, I believe that Lee would have bought one for me, but I couldn't let him spend that much money.

The coach tour finished by going to Lake Pontchartrain. Here we discovered another American 'biggest'. In this case it was the twenty-four-mile causeway that crosses the lake, 'the longest overwater highway in the world'.

Afterwards, Lee and I, feeling that we had sampled enough culture, and certainly enough hard facts about the origins of New Orleans, went around sampling a few drinks in those lovely shady courtyards. I drank whiskey-sours, a drink that Toby had introduced me to; though I didn't tell Lee that, as I have found that it never pays to discuss the merits of one man while you are out with another. I believe that they make the drink with Bourbon whiskey, bitters, lemon-juice and ice; it's a most refreshing concoction, and it has certain other good qualities too. Lee drank something that he said would be certain death to anybody but a Texan; he wouldn't tell me how it was made. It certainly seemed to have no ill effects on him, neither did it make him the least amorous, much to my surprise. In fact, in the several hours that we had spent together he never once spoke of anything concerning his intimate life, which was a pleasant change from some people I met who, in no time at all, gave me the most detailed account of their marital relations—or lack of them.

As we walked back to my hotel, I took a last sad look at the Mississippi, wishing that I could have told my family I had actually been *on* it. Certainly I never thought that I was to see it again in a very different part of the United States.

I had enjoyed my stay in New Orleans, though it seemed to me very un-American. I felt as though I were living in a foreign country where by some lucky chance all the inhabitants spoke English: an extremely pleasant foreign country, though, one in which the sun had shone and the people were laughing and friendly.

6: Grand Canyon and Las Vegas

In order to get to the Grand Canyon from New Orleans we had to fly to Las Vegas, and from there bus to a smaller airport. Toby had warned me that we would be flying in a much smaller plane, so I visualized one holding about fifty people. When I saw the size of the contraption we were to fly in, I was too astounded to speak. I simply could not believe that anybody expected us to entrust our lives to such a fragile object. There were all these so-called planes lined up on the tarmac, looking for all the world like a collection of model planes for children to play with—the kind that you wind up with an elastic band and then they zoom around for about half a minute. At first I thought that they were prototypes for some real planes—earlier designs of the Wright brothers. Perhaps ours was the original machine Alcock and Brown flew across the Atlantic. It only had room for seven people and the pilot. Once we were all in you couldn't possibly leave your seat because there was no gangway; we were packed in like sardines. However could I be so foolhardy as to think that I would survive in this mini-plane? As we taxied along the runway I closed my eyes. Had I survived the perils of the Atlantic crossing only to meet my fate in this ludicrous machine?

But the take-off was as nothing to the journey, for, as soon as the plane approached the Grand Canyon, air-currents began to rock and buffet it in a terrifying way. One minute my head was hitting the roof of the plane—admittedly it was only a foot or two above me—the next minute the plane tilted so much to one side that I thought we were going to loop the loop. I closed my eyes, inwardly saying, 'Nearer my God to thee,' alternating this with the fervent hope that 'God is my co-pilot'. But every time that I opened them I merely saw a large beefy man sitting next to the pilot and I knew that *He* wasn't. Too much imagination would be needed to see anything godlike in this companion.

I hung on grimly, consoling myself with the fact that the journey took only half an hour. So it was the last straw to hear the pilot call out cheerfully, 'There are two people on this plane who are doing the pleasure trip. All the way round the Grand Canyon. So you lucky five are coming as well; it's an hour's journey.'

All through the trip the pilot was pointing out places of interest in the canyon. Everybody got very excited at their first sight of the Boulder Dam. I know that it's a marvellous feat of engineering, but just then I couldn't have cared less if the Boulder Dam had broken up and flooded the desert.

Toby, with great forethought, had bought me a bottle of Canadian whiskey, and kept urging me to take copious swigs. He even praised me for bearing up so well, and from him that was really something; I began to feel almost a heroine. However, when the plane gave a tremendous lurch and I faintly cried, 'I bet you have never been on a trip like this,' to hear him say that he had been in three plane crashes in no way helped to boost my morale. I felt that the plane would break up any minute. And then he added, 'Think of it this way. Our men in the Battle of Britain threw their Spitfires all round the sky, and they were smaller planes than this one.'

What was the point of that? In the first place we weren't fighting a war, and secondly, any resemblance between my courage and theirs was non-existent. But inadvertently Toby did help me because I was so irritated with him by this time that I forgot my fears. Nevertheless, the relief when we landed! I felt with the poet Wordsworth, who wrote, 'Bliss was it in that dawn to be alive' except that the time was afternoon.

For a short time I was too shattered to move from the airport, but when I recovered and had my first sight of the Grand Canyon—well! How does one describe the indescribable? One can say that the Grand Canyon is colossal, awe-inspiring, majestic and mysterious, but all these superlatives have been used many times to describe far inferior places. What it needs is a new vocabulary. An astronomer, searching the heavens night after night, then miraculously finding a new planet, could not have been more entranced than I was at first seeing the Grand Canyon. It filled me with fear, and dread—not fear of falling into the abyss, but fear of the unknown, of the mortality of man. It made me feel a nothing, a minute speck in the universe. I felt as though this was the first attempt at making the world, and although it wasn't habitable, it was too wonderful to alter.

Later on I read, in the official guide, that the Grand Canyon was seven to nine million years in the making. It was caused by erosion, by the action of rain and the Colorado River on its way to the sea, plus the wind, sand and frost. But, in spite of the official explanation, it's still out of this world.

One way to get down into the canyon is to go on the mule trail. The mules are specially trained over a period of eighteen months to do this somewhat hazardous descent. The return journey takes about six hours. Toby decided to go on the mule trip, but showed extremely little enthusiasm at the idea of my accompanying him; though anyone can go as long as they are over twelve years and don't weigh more than 200 lb. He pointed out that the journey was very arduous (though I have more energy than he has) and that there were precipitous drops all the way down.

When I asked the official how safe it was, she said that in places the mule-track was only five feet wide and the mule took up four and a half feet. What a terrifying thought! Just six inches between you, a mule and eternity. Nevertheless, if I had received a little more encouragement from Toby I would have made the attempt, just to be able to say I had been *in* the canyon. I had half a mind to insist on doing the mule trip, just to see how he would cope with the situation. Probably he would have gone hot-footing it to the official to tell her that I was suffering from megalomania and would be a danger to the rest of the party.

Unknown to me, my day was already booked. Toby was always very quick and efficient at arranging things that got me out of the way. On this occasion, he booked a morning and afternoon tour by bus.

Everything here, except the Grand Canyon, seems to be owned by one man. At least, it started with one man, Fred Harvey; now it's Fred Harvey, Inc. They own the mules, buses, hotels, restaurants and gift-shops; I believe that they even own the Santa Fé Railway.

For the morning tour we all assembled outside the hotel. I took a quick look round and was surprised to see four unattached males, all round about fifty years of age. They appeared to me to be a left-over from some convention. One of the men was wearing a Stetson hat. I do think that a hat that size does something for a man. In some way it makes him look more virile. I once remarked on this to Toby, but all he said was that the size of the hat was not indicative, whatever that means, and added, 'Who cares about the hat? It's what's underneath that you want to worry about.' I don't agree. If you are not going to know the person long enough to find out what's underneath, it's nice to be able to admire the outward trappings.

One of these convention types sat next to me in the bus; he introduced himself as Charlie. 'Call me Chuck; all my friends do.' When I remarked that I could hardly be counted among his friends, having only just this moment met him, he said, in a voice that could be heard all over the bus, 'Everybody's my friend who talks to me; I love them all.'

I am not a bit keen on people who love everybody, having found through experience that such universal love results in my share of it being somewhat diluted. I much prefer individual love, even if at times it is rather over-powering.

'I love everybody' reminded me of years ago when I used to do the shopping for my mother. Every Saturday morning I went to the butcher to get the week-end joint. I always asked for the 'biggest piece of beef for two shillings'. It sounds a ludicrous sum now but I got quite a fair-sized piece of meat then. I had what I considered an undying love for our butcher, a man of about forty. He always served me himself and called me his Nelly Blythe. Never would I let anybody else serve me. But one fateful day, when I was about eleven years old, I went in as usual on a Saturday morning and one of the assistants called out, 'Here comes your sweetheart, Mr Brown.' I was thrilled to hear this, absolutely in heaven. And then came the tragedy: for Mr Brown said, 'All the girls are my sweethearts; I love them all.' Such a feeling of desolation came over me that I wanted to die. I had thought that it was me only he loved. Afterwards, I hated him. Mr Brown never did understand why I ceased to bother who served me.

To get back to Charlie. He wasn't unattractive, though somewhat gone to seed, and for my part I was glad to have somebody to talk to; though as it turned out, Charlie did most of the talking. He had been stationed in England during the last war. 'Of course I wasn't much more than twenty then,' he hastily added. He had enjoyed being in England at that time; all the girls made a terrific fuss of him; of course, the American army pay was very much higher than our men got. 'They treated me like a hero, everyone did. They needed us then; it was a different story when I went over there two years ago with my wife. A more unfriendly lot of people in our hotel I have never met. Nobody wanted to know us.' I couldn't resist pointing out that a handsome single young man would be far more likely to find a good time than a fiftyish married man, wherever he went, England or some other country. Inevitably out came the photos of his wife and children for me to admire. I never carry around any photographs of my family and if I did I wouldn't show them to strangers. Even if you thought that the wife had a face like the back of a bus you couldn't say so. Charlie showed me with great pride a snapshot of his first and only grandchild. 'Just three weeks old. Isn't he great? Weighed 9 lb 3½ oz when he was born and gains every week.' My heart sank at being on the receiving end of all these views and news of his family. The baby looked just a blob to me, as most new-born infants do. I never can understand how people can see what doesn't exist. I remember when I had my second baby, the doctor showed him to me, saying, 'There's a lovely boy for you.' What rubbish! He was as red as a boiled beetroot and wrinkled like corrugated cardboard—even the fondest of mothers couldn't have said he was lovely. Still, at least the *doctor* was young and handsome. It was his first practice and he was still full of ideals and ideas about the medical profession. 'Any time you want the baby weighed, just bring him round to the surgery; I won't charge you anything.' I thought this was marvellous. Talk about post-natal care! So at frequent intervals I'd take the baby round, lay him on the scales and then we would forget all about him until he started bawling his head off. Albert got a bit peeved sometimes, saying, 'Is the doctor giving you private lessons on bringing up children? And how much has the baby gained?' Unfortunately, I had seldom noticed this, so generally replied, 'Oh, about three to four ounces.' Of course I was flattered that somebody so elevated in social position as a doctor should notice me.

Charlie told me that years ago he had walked down to the bottom of the Grand Canyon, and found it a very strenuous trip, much harder than climbing a mountain because by the time you started to ascend the canyon you were already tired from getting down there.

There are Indians living about 2,000 feet down from the rim. They make a living by growing various crops and grazing cattle.

One of the places we stopped at was a round tower, known as the Watch Tower. It was built in 1932 by—needless to say—Fred Harvey, and is a re-creation of the real watch towers built by the Indians for storing food and as places of safety from other tribes. We all climbed to the top to admire the view and Charlie gave a running commentary on the points of interest. I was already somewhat sorry that I had been so friendly with him, because if there is one thing that you can do without at the Grand Canyon, it is conversation. It is not a place for chatter; it is too beautiful, too overwhelming. I made up my mind that in the afternoon trip I would not speak to anybody on the bus.

As it happened, over the lunch I sat next to an elderly lady who introduced herself in the friendliest possible way as a Mrs Moore from Indiana. It would have been churlish not to speak to her and really would have made her think that the English were stand-offish. She was a widow and was seeing something of her own country before she got too old to travel; she had lived all her life in Indiana. She asked me about England. How does one tell a stranger about one's own country? Especially as, even after these few weeks, England seemed so remote and America so very much with me. I tried to explain London to her—no real skyscrapers; lovely parks and shops; full of Americans doing the city—when they could spare the time from searching Plymouth for records of their ancestors who came over in the *Mayflower*. (A well-known American once wrote that the *Mayflower* must either have been a floating city or made innumerable trips between England and America to accommodate all the people who made the crossing.) Mrs Moore and I found a common interest in books, especially when I told her that the American, Henry James, was one of my favourite authors, though he lived in England far more than in America.

For the afternoon bus trip we went to all the official viewing-points. These are all railed in, but even so I could not help shuddering at the immense depths below. In places I could see the Colorado River and could even see the rapids, as it was such a clear day; I fancied that I could even hear them too.

I cannot with any accuracy describe this strange and awesome place—the colours, rose-red, deep purple and mauve; the fantastic formations; the enormous red cliffs; the pinnacles of rock. There are rock formations that resemble Eastern temples—two are named Vishnu and Wotan—another is just like an amphitheatre of ancient Greece. Farther on was a wedding cake, tiers of red and blue-grey, castles and plateaux. Mile after mile, the Grand Canyon covers an area two hundred miles long by thirteen miles wide. And everywhere are the brilliant, red precipitous cliffs. Mrs Moore and I stood and stared and listened to our very knowledgeable and pleasant guide, and we never spoke a word, because words would have been an intrusion.

When I got back to the hotel I was as exhausted as though I had physically traversed those rocks. Our hotel was very comfortable, ranch-style, and blended well with the scenery and landscape.

One thing that I could not get used to was the smallness of American baths. They seem to have been designed for a race of midgets. I suppose it's because Americans have no time, or desire, to loll around soaking in the water. They use the showers. These are fine once you have discovered how to regulate the flow so that you are not alternately scalded or frozen, or shot out of the bath by the velocity of the cataract of water.

I expected to find Toby when I got back to the hotel. I was even optimistic enough to think that he might be looking out for me and feeling some compunction at having left me alone all day. What a hope! There wasn't a sign of him until much later. He was resting after his arduous day—six hours on the back of a mule. I believe he thought it as much of a feat as climbing Everest—I wonder what the mule thought! When eventually he showed up, barely able to walk, all he wanted to do was sit in the lounge and watch television. It was an ice-hockey match between Boston and the Rangers. By the excitement this match seemed to generate I thought it was the Cup Final. Toby said that I should watch this ice-hockey, as it was a typical American game and this in particular was a decisive match. I hadn't the slightest desire to watch, as I was completely ignorant of the rules of the game and Toby wasn't prepared to explain them to me. All I could understand was that at frequent intervals the players fought with each other in a free for all, for what reason I hadn't a clue. Fortunately, a very charming young American, seeing my bewilderment, took the trouble to explain just how ice-hockey was played. After that, I too became quite excited and even had a bet with him on the result. And I won my dollar, too. Nothing to the game once you know the rules; I wish I'd bet five dollars.

Afterwards Toby and I had dinner with him and his wife. They really were two of the nicest Americans that I met, so full of genuine interest in our journey.

In this hotel there were several cowboy-type men. They reminded me of old-time westerns where women were few and far between. Consequently, as they had rarity value, the men cherished them, and were chivalrous, not as they seem to be now, continually assessing a woman's qualifications as a bed-mate. Probably they were too tired after lassoing cattle all day.

Next day, we were leaving for Las Vegas, so I got up at 5.30 a.m. to see the sun rise over the Grand Canyon. It was an unforgettable scene. I filled my eyes, my brain and my imagination with this unique experience; I wanted it to seep into me.

Toby came out shortly afterwards, but we did not speak to each other, for neither of us wanted to speak. People kept passing by, but I would not look at them; all that I wanted to do was to gaze at the incredible beauty and wonder as the sun steadily lit up those spires and magic palaces. If I never again gaze at the Grand Canyon I shall always consider it a privilege to have been there and shall treasure for evermore the wonder and the silence, above all the silence, which is almost a tangible thing, far, far removed from the rackety noise of the gambling machines at Las Vegas airport: that was tangible enough. And the machines were nearly all in use. There was a girl money-changer there; she told me that one is on duty all the time.

This is a country for machines. One seems to be able to get practically everything from them—tea, coffee, biscuits and cheese, paper tissue handkerchiefs. I even got a carton of tomato soup. Mind you, it was like no tomato soup that I have ever tasted; nevertheless, it was liquid and it was hot. The nicest thing about American machines is that they work. You put in your cents, press the appropriate button, and always something comes out. It may not be what you wanted, or what you hoped to get; still you haven't paid something for nothing. They are unlike some of our machines which seem to me to be merely receptacles for giving money to the government, as though they don't take enough in tax. Times without number I have put my five- or ten-new-pence piece in the stamp-machine after the post office has closed, only to find that nothing happens. No stamp, no returned coin. In fury I bang the object, then spend more pence the following day going to the post office to get back my money. As for the telephones, words fail me. On one occasion I put in a ten-pence piece, and, getting no answer, I telephoned the operator. 'You shouldn't put in ten pence to start with,' she said. 'Put in two pence, then you can't lose so much.' What a system that expects you to lose from the start!

At Las Vegas, even although the machines worked, they also expected you to lose from the start. I was later told that the payment was only eighty per cent. For every dollar put in, only eighty cents came back.

We had booked in at the International Hilton Hotel. What a place! Kubla Khan's pleasure dome could not have been much more opulent, and at first sight it certainly seemed as though it covered 'twice five miles of fertile ground'. It was vast, a prodigal display of wealth to the eye and a soporific to the mind, inducing a feeling of indifference to real life.

I knew that Las Vegas was a gambling city, but in my wildest dreams I never imagined that it was like this. I thought that people went out to play at casinos, but every hotel is a casino. This hotel, enormous, lush, deep-carpeted, ablaze with light from dozens of chandeliers, with so many staff that there seemed to be one to every two guests, simply overwhelmed me, while at the same time it gave me a feeling of hopeless depression. Here, in this hotel, were thousands of pounds being frittered away on an empty useless pursuit. The contrast between the grandeur, wonder and peace of the Grand Canyon, all made by nature, and this vast man-made, florid and ornate hotel was almost unbelievable. To me it appeared like a modern Babylon, just as incomprehensible as the biblical one. One didn't have to be an advocate of the underprivileged and deprived; one didn't have to consider the starving in India or the homeless refugees in any country ravaged by war, to feel some sense of incredulity at all this ceaseless gambling, twenty-four hours a day. There were hundreds of machines, taking anything from five cents to a dollar; there were roulette tables, baccarat, American craps and other gambling games unknown to me. Automatic and systematic robbery, it seemed—not robbing in the legal sense, but robbery in that these lush surroundings removed you not only from your money—and that happened all the time—but removed you from any feeling that you were playing a losing game.

What was even more depressing was that nobody looked happy. They didn't smile, or laugh out loud, or look as though they were having a good time. On every face there seemed to be a fixed, grim and determined expression. They looked as though this perpetual process was a form of penance that they had to fulfil for an unforgiveable sin—a matter of life or death.

All this was on the ground floor of the hotel and when I tell you that they advertised five other restaurants and a large section for bingo, as well as bars and shops, you can imagine the size of the hotel. Everything was so arranged that you had to pass the casino to reach wherever you wanted to go, because if you stopped to have a go at only one machine, it was more grist to the mill.

Toby was just as depressed as I was at the contrast between this and the Grand Canyon that we had just left. We were very glad that we had only a twenty-four hour stay.

As every hotel on what is known as the 'Strip' was, according to Toby, exactly the same as the one we were in, we decided to remain in ours for the evening. We could have gone to Caesar's Palace to hear Tom Jones, but although I like to hear him sing I hadn't travelled all these miles to hear him in another country. Or there was the Folies Bergère at the Tropicana Hotel, or a singing group at the Frontier Hotel.

We managed to locate the English Bar which was about as English as a French bistro, inasmuch as the first thing that we asked for, English beer, was not, never had been and never would be in stock. 'It doesn't travel well,' the barman said. 'Not even in cans. Have our beer, it's just the same. And we do serve it properly, good and cold. All the beer in England is lukewarm.' People came out with remarks like this the whole time. Some of our beer is served lukewarm I'll admit, but not all of it. In any case, though I have nothing against American beer, it isn't the same as ours. And why call it the English Bar when you can't get an English drink?

Toby got into conversation with a man at the bar who turned out to be a Texan oil millionaire. He did not even bother to gamble in person but did it all by proxy; one of the casino girls came up every so often to give him his winnings or collect more money. He lost considerably more than he won, but with all his wealth I suppose the loss made little difference. Contrary to my idea that an oil millionaire would be interested only in making money, this Texan was a very well-read and knowledgeable man, a geologist. He told us that years ago, when he drilled for his first oil-well, it cost only thirty thousand dollars and from the start of the oil being produced it made two hundred pounds per day. Now he had oil-wells everywhere. He only leased the land, but as he had seven-eighths of the profits it was easy to see why he was a millionaire.

In this atmosphere, Toby and I decided to lose a little of our money, if only to say that we too had gambled at Las Vegas. We did lose it too, though Toby was lucky on the gambling machines. When *I* won I laughed out loud, which is certainly not the done thing. I put one five-cent piece in and got five out. I said to the woman at the next machine, 'I must have beginner's luck.' She looked at me as though I were a being from another planet, and never said a word.

How different it is when Albert and I go into a pub and have a go on the fruit machine! If we start to win, people gather round and cheer and it makes a friendly evening. Did these people cheer here? Not on your life. They were as lifeless as the very machines engorging their money.

Very soon after dinner we decided we might as well give up and retire for the night. But I could not sleep. Even high above as I was I imagined that I could still hear the hum from below. I think that my brain was too full of all I had seen; so at 2.30 a.m. I went down to see if the scene had changed. Surely they must go to bed sometimes? Well, if they did, others must have taken their places for there were still as many people about. I wandered into the coffee shop where I did manage to get into conversation with a peroxided woman wearing diamanté-framed spectacles and looking about as benevolent as a starving vulture. She was taking a breather from her main occupation, gambling. She told me that she was celebrating her second divorce and was spending the huge settlement that she had wheedled out of her ex-husband— well, it seemed huge in dollars. Without blinking an eyelid she informed me that she had already lost, in two days, five hundred dollars, and that she was staying in the hotel another four days.

'So what will you do when all the money has gone?'

'I'll find another mug to get married to. There's plenty around.'

I thought that surely no man would take her on. But perhaps when she wasn't gambling she became human again.

'As you are staying here for a few days you will have time to see something of Las Vegas,' I remarked. She looked at me in astonishment.

'See Las Vegas! Who wants to see Las Vegas? Everything that I want is right here in this hotel. I don't come here for the scenery; I can get plenty of that elsewhere.'

'Does it make you happy to come here and gamble?'

'Happy! What's happy? Who cares about happy? I come here for the excitement. I feel really alive here; it does for me what drink does for some people.'

It costs a lot more, I thought, but remained silent, as I'm sure she thought my questions idiotic.

She went off to get another shot of excitement and I looked around to see if there was another person prepared to take a break from being parted from his money. I tried to imagine just what it must cost to run a hotel like this, with five restaurants—

99

or it could have been six—as well as bars and coffee shops, and every comfort that could be devised. They must employ hundreds of servants, on duty day and night. Some time afterwards I read in an American newspaper that an average big hotel in Las Vegas must take in 125,000 dollars each day to break even. The amount that they took from Toby and me didn't help much.

There seemed to be a lot more middle-aged women than any other people. Perhaps they were widows, or their husbands, unable to stay the course, had retired to bed. Women in America do seem to have a lot more stamina than the men. Perhaps it is because the men work very hard, to ensure that their wives don't have to do so. These women looked as though a great deal of money was spent on them—blue-rinsed and elaborately waved hair, very expensively dressed, lots of jewellery and a general air of 'I have been here before'.

I got into conversation with one woman in a coffee shop. She explained to me, with that lack of reticence that I found in many Americans—only *they* see it as being friendly and warm-hearted —that American men look upon love as they do the making of money. They have to go on making the latter in order to have an adequate supply of the former.

'Once they get a wife,' she went on, 'they lose interest in the physical side of marriage. They regard a wife as a show-piece, deck her in jewels, set her in an expensive house or apartment. She can then be the visible evidence of just how wealthy is the husband.'

When I said that Englishmen were not rated as great lovers, she went on, 'Perhaps not, but from what I heard about English women they place no value on themselves as wives. They don't convey the idea that the husband is lucky to get a wife. An American woman's idea of love is that she confers a favour on a man by marrying him, that she has made a sacrifice. Consequently Americans treasure their wives as much as they do the money that they make.'

I was constantly to hear that we do not understand or appreciate the American way of life. But honestly, they have an equally distorted view about us in England.

I had another go on the fruit machines and lost three dollars, which was enough for me. Each side of me were ladies feverishly and for ever pulling the handles, up and down, as though they were engaged in some rite which demanded this form of energy. And like Sisyphus for ever rolling his stone up the mountain, and for ever seeing it roll down again, they too, with their plastic cups of cents for ever fed the insatiable machines until the cup was empty. Then could the victims leave, having propitiated the machine? Not so. Like zombies, they walked as in a dream to the money-changing booth and changed their dollar bills for more cents, and repeated the process.

I went in for more coffee and sat down next to a very elderly gentleman who looked to me as though he should have been in bed hours ago. He was a pleasant man and actually listened while I was telling him my impressions of this vast hotel and the gambling.

'Don't judge America by this scene,' he said. 'This is no more America, and these no more typical Americans, than Lapland and the Eskimos.'

He really was very funny in his dry comments on the people around, calling them the torpid troglodytes. 'As for my wife, she would never go to bed at all if she could help it. That's her over there at the roulette table, the blonde lady in the pink dress— what there is of it.' Well, she must have been at least forty years younger than her husband. No wonder she never wanted to go to bed.

'Why don't *you* go to bed?' I asked him. 'You look worn out. Do you gamble as well as your wife?'

'Not likely; she can lose money fast enough for two. If I were to do the same we would be able to stay here only a day or two instead of a week, and that would infuriate Sally. I stay down here just in case she wins at the roulette table and gets ideas of trying something with even higher stakes.'

But he was very philosophical about Las Vegas, saying that if people had money to burn they might as well get rid of it in comfort. Certainly they could spend it on far more worthy causes, but one must remember that for some of the people at the tables and machines this was a once-in-a-lifetime spree. They might have gone without a holiday for years just to have this one fling. Perhaps he was right. But as it was now 5 a.m. I had one final look at the scene and went back to bed.

Thinking of the whole scene as I lay awake reminded me of a recurrent dream I have, of a vast concourse of people. I can see and hear them but can establish no contact. I go from one to the other touching them, but they do not feel, see or hear me. I am aware of this and it is frightening and macabre. I felt that all I had seen here was like a waking dream.

I felt a great sense of relief to know that I would not be in Las Vegas for another night.

7: Los Angeles

After surviving the perils of that journey across the Grand Canyon, I actually welcomed the sight of the plane that was to fly us from Las Vegas to Los Angeles. At least it was a proper size.

But I did often wish, during my weeks in America, that I could have had enough time to travel on a long bus or train journey and really get to know my fellow-travellers. Nobody seems to bother about conversation on a plane; they eat and drink, read the newspapers and books, or just go to sleep. Travelling across America by bus I would have seen so much more of the country. I could have seen it in detail instead of just as a blurred mass from the air. Then there would have been lots of wayside stops for refreshment and different people to see and talk to; and as for my fellow-passengers, I'm sure we would have all got to be old friends by the time the journey was over. I would have felt that I really 'knew' America personally instead of rushing over it.

Los Angeles being a city so well-known in England, mainly because of films and television, I gazed eagerly around on the journey from the airport. The view was grim: nothing but concrete roads teeming with traffic. These motorways, or freeways as they are called here, are an absolute necessity, but I should think that to an inexperienced driver they must be a nightmare. They are four-laned and you must not slow down or stop. In theory you should keep to sixty-five miles an hour, but in practice, as a coach-driver told us, you must keep up with the traffic in front. You are as likely to get a ticket for going too slowly as for going too fast. But without the freeways, I don't know how people would get in and out of the city.

I have read so much about this State of California, of Los Angeles and Hollywood: of all the American states, I think that California has been most written about as an example of a modern Utopia: indeed it has been called the Golden State. The climate is one of the best in the world, and the scenery is wonderful: mountains, lovely valleys and always sunshine. But although it was thought to be the perfect setting for the American dream, disillusionment seems to have crept in with the hippies, drugs and violence. One American wrote, 'This paradise on earth is now a hell, a fairy tale with a nightmare ending; mutilated and ruined by the very people who originally moved in to this Promised Land.'

Was it ever a paradise except for the wealthy? I was determined to see for myself as much as I possibly could.

Los Angeles is certainly not a city for pedestrians; everything that you want to see is so widely separated. The city sprawls for ever and, in fact, does cover some 453 square miles. I reckon that in the few days I was there I managed to go over only the odd fifty-three miles—a mere nothing.

Los Angeles was once just an Indian village, then known as Jong-na. Now it's the fourth largest city in the United States, with a population of over two and a half million.

We had booked in to Hyatt House Hotel on Sunset Boulevard, right on the part known as the Strip. I had a lovely room but unfortunately, as I was so high up, I couldn't use the balcony. Waking at three o'clock the following morning I stood there for a few minutes, but I experienced a dreadful feeling that it would break away and hurtle to the depths below, carrying me with it. I hastily retreated to my room; the window faced a large expanse of Los Angeles. It was shimmering with lights, very enticing and alluring. This blaze of light seemed to have nothing to do with the city; it hung there suspended in space like some ethereal palace of dreams. The boulevard was empty and quiet.

I was like a cat on hot bricks in my desire to get out and about, so I was up and had finished my breakfast by eight o'clock on this first morning. I knew that it would be fatal to the enjoyment of the day to ring Toby's room before nine o'clock, in view of his annoyance at being wakened at what he calls an unearthly hour. So I wandered out on to Sunset Boulevard. I was under orders from my mum to do this, and I am nearly as scared of her as I am of Toby. I knew that I daren't go back and say I hadn't bothered to walk on it. Mum would want a detailed account of what it looked like. She went to films about three times a week in the old silent film days and she believes that Hollywood is full of glamorous ladies parading up and down the boulevard, dripping with jewels and furs. If she could have seen it as I did that morning I'm sure it would have been a shock enough to hasten her departure from this world; for what with the traffic, the motels, the sleazy shows, glamour was no more—if indeed it ever was there.

When I returned to the hotel, was Toby up and about? Not on your life. He was nowhere to be seen or heard. What a way of going on! I feel just as happy when I get up as at any other time. When he eventually appeared, however, arrangements had been made to visit Disneyland. When I discovered that Toby had included himself in these arrangements, I was delighted. But this pleasure was premature.

What a fantastic place it is! One drives for miles along the ugly grim freeways when suddenly, as one turns off, there is this amazing place which cannot be seen from the road; it appears to spring from nowhere. What struck me at first was its hygienic and aseptic appearance. Here was this vast crowd of people, hundreds of children, and not a bit of paper or rubbish to be seen. Then I realized that there was a huge number of employees continually going around with long-handled dustpans and brushes sweeping up even such small things as bus-tickets. It certainly bore no resemblance to our Battersea Fun Fair, where all the débris of day-trippers litters the ground. Lunch-bags, cigarette-packets, ice-cream cartons are cheerfully discarded and trodden under foot. We English may be clean and fussy in our homes, but a foreigner seeing our railway stations, trains and public places would have a nasty shock. But somehow Disneyland seemed to me too clean, too much of a show-place; if there were magic there, it didn't work for me. Perhaps one needed to be a child who still believed in fairyland, or a teenager who would have fun trying out the various amusements such as the monorail trip to the moon or the flying planes.

Mind you, I would have enjoyed it more with the right companion, but Toby was a dead loss in such a place; I don't know why on earth he came. If it really was to please me, as I had imagined it was, then why not disguise his only too obvious disparagement, and at least make an effort on my behalf. I was rapidly coming to the conclusion that Toby thought this trip to America was all for his benefit. He instantly summed Disneyland up as nothing but a commercial proposition.

One needs to be able to suspend belief in the real world and accept this pictorial representation. But with a companion who all the time was bursting the bubble, what chance had I? I would have liked to have tried a trip to the moon or gone on the jungle river, but I was afraid to go off on my own in case I lost Toby. He might just have wandered off, and all hopes of finding our coach for the trip back would have gone. He only wanted to do the things that required no effort at all, such as sitting in a hall watching a life-like model represent Abraham Lincoln, or in an old-time picture-house watching five screens, all showing extremely ancient silent pictures, all of which I had already seen on television in England.

Why didn't I protest? I don't know. I certainly would have done back in England. But I suffered all the time from a feeling that at any moment he might disappear. He seemed to me like a genie from a bottle, and unless I placated him and kept him in sight all the time, he would vanish in a puff of smoke. Whenever I came back from a coach trip, it was always with a sense of pleasurable shock that I found him still around.

Nevertheless, from what I saw of Disneyland, it is a paradise for children, though perhaps a somewhat expensive one, as money is needed for almost everything there.

You enter first of all into a village square and find yourself in a typical Main Street of an American small town complete with horse-drawn fire brigade, drink saloon and brass band, with all the attendants in the appropriate costumes. Farther on there is Frontier Land, with Davy Crockett, covered-wagons and Indians whooping around, and everything to remind an American of his country's past history. Although I'm not an American, I still found it fascinating and could have spent hours watching the scene.

Talking about this to an American back in the hotel, I found that he too, like Toby, was somewhat lukewarm about the whole concept. He reckoned that it was never built for children at all; their amusements were only an after-thought. 'It's there for those Americans who find the present too awful to live in. So they spend their spare time in a place like Disneyland, revelling in a make-believe world of old-time heroes and pioneers, of the simple life in a small town, of wresting a living from the soil. None of that Disneyland history is real; it's just a re-creation of how Americans want life to be.'

'Surely you are making social implications out of what, after all, is just one vast amusement park?' I asked.

'Not at all. Americans don't look on it like that. To them it's their lost childhood. They see it as the vanished good life, the American dream before it became the American nightmare. They would like to go right back to those days, back to the Puritans and the pioneers.'

'But not back to the Red Indians?' I said. There was silence after that. But it was obvious that this remark about the Indians rankled with him, for he gazed at me for what seemed like five minutes, saying nothing at all. Then he suddenly said, apropos of nothing that I could see, 'Well now, have you any other old junk that you can send over here? You have already sold to us your old London Bridge, the *Queen Mary* and the *Queen Elizabeth*. Maybe you'd like to sell us Ireland; you don't seem to have much use for it.'

I too was as silent after this as he had been over the Indians. I found that some Americans had extremely distorted views about Ireland, looking on our role there as a traitorous one. The newspaper, *Las Vegas Sun*, printed a letter from a correspondent who wrote, 'The whole world knows that England invaded and took over little Ireland several hundred years ago. The Irish were forced to leave their country and were shipped to practically every corner of the world. A great percentage died on board ship from starvation and disease.' There was lots more of this in the same strain. On thinking about it I suppose some English people are equally unbalanced about the Americans' role in Vietnam.

One of the hazards of being in a foreign country where they spoke the same language as us was finding that what made me laugh was not necessarily funny to them. Conversely, when I heard jokes about their coming election, I couldn't see the point. My remark about the Indians was not meant to be serious; I did not then realize how some Americans feel about the original inhabitants: that they have feelings of guilt about what happened in the past. So I hastily changed the subject of Indians and Irish and remarked to him, 'I'm sure you will agree with me that Los Angeles is no city for walking; there is nowhere to go which is near enough. Everything has to be reached by bus or car. I should think that people here will soon lose the use of their legs.' With this sentiment we were in perfect agreement.

Nobody seemed actually to live in the city. All I could see were hotels, motels, shops, restaurants and theatres. I suppose that accounts for the cars; people came into the centre but lived in the suburbs.

Here on Sunset Boulevard were the usual sex shows. From my hotel window I could see a sign that advertised, 'Just one nude, the rest are stark naked'. A typical American joke. When I walked past, they were also advertising an amateur nude contest. Perhaps that meant that the female who removed her clothes in the most elegant manner got the prize. A rival establishment, not to be outdone, proclaimed 'topless and bottomless'. I wondered what they wore in the middle. There were also '12 sinful sisters'. Surely no family could have twelve girls; or if they did they wouldn't all be sinful. Judging by the pictures outside, the sisters had been knocking around for a good many years.

I could just imagine the look on my mum's face if she could have seen these establishments. In fact, just to give her the most up-to-date information about Sunset Strip I even wondered whether I should go to look at one of these shows, but I decided that *that* sacrifice would be too great, as well as too boring. For one thing it would have been bread and bread. For another I could see just as good—or bad—in Soho.

Nevertheless there was one coach trip I definitely had to be on if I didn't want my mum's reproaches when I returned. I knew that a visit to Hollywood and the Universal Studios was a must; Mum would definitely require a detailed account of it. She never looked upon the stars as pasteboard characters, but implicitly believed in the goodness of the heroes, and the evil and violence of the villains.

I quite expected to find a coach-load of 'Mums', all wanting to see where the old-time epics were made, so I was surprised to find as many young as old. I hadn't realized that, although very few films are made there nowadays, the studios are used for television, especially the 'series', and the young people wanted to see it all for that reason.

A spry little old woman who sat next to me confided that she was eighty-six—she certainly didn't look it—and that she was thrilled, simply thrilled, to think that she was going to be where all the famous film-stars had once trod. She loved them all and thought that this new lot weren't half as good as the old. With great alacrity I attached myself to her; I thought she would be a mine of information—and I was quite right too. When I told her that my mum was nearly ninety-two and absolutely doted on all the old film-stars, this Emily really let herself go so that I could relate it all to Mum. Why, she was thirty or so when she first saw Lillian Gish in *Orphans of the Storm* and she cried all the time in there and all the way home, and the starched collar of her muslin blouse was all limp with the tears that had fallen on it. And when she got back to the farm her husband—God rest his soul, he had been dead for twenty-five years—said that she was a great fool and if she wanted to weep over someone let her weep and pray for him and for the rain. But he was a good man at heart, it was just the hard work and no rain and the cows dying which made him lose heart and become bitter. But underneath it all he was still fond of her. This torrent of information poured out of her like water from a broken dam. All I had to do was make sympathetic noises at intervals. Privately I gathered the impression that the departed husband was a disagreeable old curmudgeon who hung on to life and showed no desire to take off for a better time in the next world unless he could take Emily too, to keep on nagging at her.

In one way, for Emily and for me too, this visit to the film studios was one long sequence of disillusionment. For we were shown how many of the scenes and events in the old films were really made. I am not so naïve that I didn't know a lot of the daring and adventure was faked, but to see how the public were so easily fooled was a bit much. We saw burning houses that were just the front part with cans of some liquid fixed to the back and realistic 'flames' coming through the windows; trees that fell down and then were pulled up as we passed; torrents of water bursting down the road, that also ceased as we got by; great, presumably cardboard, rocks hurtling down and mysteriously going up the mountain afterwards; miles of rocky and desert scenery going past the cowboys—instead of them riding through it. I tell you, 'You can fool all the people all of the time.' Nevertheless, it was enjoyable. We saw the dressing-rooms of the television stars and afterwards watched a demonstration of how the stunt men do their seemingly impossible deeds—like falling off the roof of a house. In this case, they fell backwards on to a mattress; but it was still risky as the house was high and the mattress exceedingly small by comparison.

In spite of this tour of official disillusionment, Emily would not believe that her old-time heroes and heroines were like that. 'It's all these modern so-called stars,' she said; 'they haven't the guts or stamina of the old lot. They were the real kind of film-stars, out to entertain the public.' I couldn't help thinking that Mum would agree with her, and it's very few people that my mum agrees with nowadays.

We all went then to the Hollywood Cemetery where, among many others, Rudolph Valentino is buried. Some of the women openly wept over his grave but, as he was never a hero of mine, it left me unmoved. I remember seeing him in *The Sheik* and *Blood and Sand*, but his particular brand of masculinity never appealed to me; it was too far from reality. Besides, I could not believe that sheiks were desirable lovers, even if they were passionate. The sanitary arrangements of those primitive countries would not have had much to recommend them. However much in love you are, the realities of life are always there.

The coach drove through Beverly Hills to show us the style in which the stars live. There were magnificent houses, each in its own grounds, hidden among trees and shrubs, and invisible from the freeways. No cars are allowed to speed; in fact the limit is twenty miles an hour. I went through there one night and it was so quiet that one could hardly believe that all the noise of the city was so near. But although this was such a lovely place, such displays of wealth must surely bring about a certain amount of worry and anxiety with so much crime in the city. Across the top of a page in one day's *Los Angeles Times* was 'W. Hollywood pays for its Glamour with Crime'. It went on to say that this community, with Sunset Strip, had one of the highest crime-rates in the country, and that in burglary it was No. 1. So it can't be all honey to live in an expensive apartment or house; often one must be afraid to open the door, especially in the evening.

On the way back the coach stopped at Grauman's Chinese Theatre, that holy of holies where countless stars of the screen have left their footprints, not 'in the sands of time', but in the cement forecourt. What a marvel actually to see your pin-up's footprint—nobody has ever wanted to inspect mine! We all descended from the coach at this very colourful and exotic-looking picture-house and solemnly inspected the foot-prints and signatures. Everybody bent down under imminent risk of slipped discs or some other spinal disorder. Afterwards, back in the hotel, I wondered what had got into me that I should indulge in such a puerile pursuit, as I couldn't really care less about film-stars and in the normal way wouldn't cross the road to inspect their footprints or even them themselves. Now if only Mum could have been there, she would probably have got right down and kissed the ground they had walked on. What an old fans' reunion she and Emily could have had! They could have wept on each other's shoulders, remembering all the pathetic heroines they had loved. Emily said that she was too old to bend her back so she would have to get down on her knees. But this didn't deter her; she had come prepared with a small cushion to kneel on. I told her, 'Don't worry; I'll read out the names to you,' but Emily would have none of that. 'Never could I go back home and say that I hadn't with my own eyes seen all this evidence of the famous. Why, my sister would never forgive me. She too wanted to come, but the doctor said she was too old to bus around all over the country. Sarah was furious with him; says she is going to change her doctor. She knows better than he does just what she can, and can't do.'

'How old is Sarah, then?' I asked with some amusement.

'Oh, a bit older than me—ninety-one.' I got the impression that Sarah, just like my mum, refuses to face the fact that old age has at last caught up with her.

I enjoyed talking to Emily. She was a fund of information about the early days in the Mid West of America and how hard everybody worked and how good-neighbourly people were. Even the poorest, who couldn't help financially when disaster fell, gave of their time freely.

On the way back to the city centre along the freeways, I noticed the concentration of our driver. Just like the taxi-driver from the airport, he kept his eyes firmly fixed on the car in front, looking neither to right or left. To the uninitiated, the roads must appear like a maze, and even to a driver who knows the freeways, as our driver did, there can be no pleasure in thus rushing along.

Before the earth was torn to pieces to make these motorways, before the grass became concrete and the trees overhead signs, Los Angeles must have been a beautiful place. Of course, it still is in places, but not in the city itself.

Yet the following morning, the day before we were to leave Los Angeles, when I got into conversation with an American from New York, he reckoned that the traffic problem there was by far the worst. 'It's absolute chaos in New York, in the rush hours; you can sit in your car for ever, unable to move. At least here in Los Angeles they do have a system of some kind, however grim it looks.'

He introduced himself as Mr Morrison. At least the name sounded like that, but he was chewing a large lump of waffle at the time. He told me that he was having breakfast on his own because his wife was still in bed, not very well.

'She's not herself, not herself at all.'

At frequent intervals during our conversation, and he did most of the talking, he would interrupt himself to say, 'My wife's not herself at all.' By the time that I had heard this on some half-dozen occasions, I was tempted to enquire, 'Well, who is she, then?'

Mr Morrison was the chief of some public concern in New York; I never did understand just what it was. Within five minutes of my knowing him, he also told me that he was Jewish.

What makes some Jews feel that they have to assert this fact? Of what importance is it? People don't come up and say, 'I'm a Catholic,' or 'I'm a Protestant.' Do they find that being Jewish makes them separate, unique, superior, the Chosen People? I remember once having an argument with a Jewish family for whom I worked. They told me how many past and present famous figures in politics, art and business had been Jewish. But, as I replied, it wasn't being Jewish that made them eminent: they would have been clever whatever they were.

This American began to tell me the history of his family, going back generations, and how his grandparents came to America to escape the pogroms in Poland. I know that the pogroms were numerous, but sometimes I cannot help feeling that surely some of the emigrants must have left for other reasons, so many times have I listened to similar stories. It does seem to be a prestige thing to have Polish grandparents and a pogrom.

Mr Morrison was somewhat contemptuous of President Nixon and his blockade of Hanoi and Haiphong. 'There's nothing to it,' he said, 'it's just an election gimmick to make sure he is re-elected. As soon as ever the election is over, Nixon will have the troops out of Vietnam in no time.'

I asked him if the President was popular. 'He is here in the West, because he was born here. In New York we don't think anything of him. He's selling our country to the blacks who, he says, are under-privileged and deprived, but who have kids by the dozen that my taxes have to keep.'

When I somewhat timidly interrupted this tirade to mention that the blacks had to live in awful houses, he got really angry.

'Whose fault is that? They are given decent places to live in and what happens? They all congregate and make their own ghettoes or garbage.'

I was horrified to listen to the venom and animosity in his voice, especially as I had seen some of these soul-destroying slums.

It was hopeless to try to change the view point of a man so fixed in his opinions. But still I did go on, 'If they don't have children, what have they got? Having a family must be about the only way that they can feel any sense of identity.'

He would have none of this, saying that our Jamaicans and

West Indians were as angels compared to their blacks. He was equally furious about the rioting and demonstrating students.

Toby and I had already heard a similar view from the taxi-driver who drove us from the airport. The students had rioted the day before we arrived. The taxi-driver was ranting. 'We are too damn soft with them. In any other country but America they would be shot.' We promptly said, 'They certainly wouldn't be shot in England. Not even put into prison as they are here.'

When I said as much to Mr Morrison, all I heard was, 'We all know the Unions run your country, and the Unions are run by Communists. The pity is that you haven't a McCarthy to root them out. But you are all too soft over there, now that Churchill's gone.'

I was far from sorry when eventually he left to see if Mrs Morrison was still not herself. I was not surprised at her indisposition, married to such a man as he; I shouldn't think that she ever got the chance to be herself.

I sat there finishing my breakfast. Depression hung over me like a cloud until another man came up to me and said, 'You are Margaret Powell, aren't you?'

When I nodded gloomily, he went on, 'I thought that I wasn't mistaken. I have often heard you on the radio in England. To hear your voice in Los Angeles is like manna from heaven.'

Wasn't that a most heart-warming and charming thing to say? It's the first time in my life that anybody has compared my voice to manna from heaven. I went up to my room feeling much happier, turned on the television, and before the picture came on heard a most seductive man's voice saying, 'You are not getting older; you are getting better.' That really made my day. I hastily turned off the television before the illusion was dispelled.

Reading a newspaper in my room I found out that this city's name, Los Angeles, means, 'The village of Our Lady, Queen of the Angels of Porcuincula'. I had always understood it to mean Lost Angels, which would have certainly been more appropriate, judging by what I could see from my hotel window on Sunset Boulevard. I must admit that daylight had soon dispelled my earlier vision of Los Angeles as a dream city. All I could see in the morning was a pall of smog.

I wish that I had had time to visit such beautiful parts as the San Fernando Valley and some of the lovely beaches. I had imagined that in Los Angeles I would hear the waves breaking on the shore; why, I couldn't even see the sea, not even from my high window—perhaps the smog obscured the view. But even so, in the hills, it was easy to forget the vulgarity and garishness of the Strip, and the roar of the traffic on the freeways. No wonder that the film industry flourished here in Hollywood. The scenery and climate were already laid on.

During my few days I saw quite a few empty spaces advertised as vacant lots for building. I was continually amazed at the speed with which things get done in America. One saw miles of road dug up one day to lay cables; the next day it was all back again to its original state. It's as though the work in England is done by two men and a shovel, while the Americans use a hundred men and fast-moving equipment.

An American, who travels to England every year, told me, 'You know what? When I was over in your country two years ago the road was up right by your Buckingham Palace. Last year, when I went back, it was still up.' I tried to explain to him that for some unknown reason the powers that be had an irresistible urge to dig holes in the road; that it was fast becoming a national pastime, especially in the summer months when London was full of visitors to be inconvenienced by this peculiarity of ours. We consider our holes such an attraction for tourists that we even provide viewing points for them. As I told him, that particular hole had probably been dug out and filled in several times during his absence.

A girl-friend of mine nearly became engaged to a hole-digger. As befits such arduous work, her Bill was a hefty fellow with great bulging muscles like bladders of lard. He was born in some remote village where there were only six families who had all intermarried—practically incest, it seemed to me. Bill had left the village because there was no work there. But, as he told us, he had to be near to the earth, and the nearest that he could get to it in London was to dig it up and put it back again. He had two stock phrases that he was everlastingly bringing out. The first was 'You must take me as you find me.' I know what that means. It's just an excuse for not bothering to dress up or be polite. The second saying of his, 'I'm just a simple son of the soil,' was certainly true as far as the 'simple' was concerned. At twenty-one he still read all the kids' comics, and his favourite game was snakes and ladders. And as though he wasn't already hefty enough, he went to weight-lifting classes twice a week.

I said to Mary, 'However can you think of marrying Bill? By the time that you've gazed at those muscles and that hairy chest every night, in between playing snakes and ladders and hearing him bellowing with glee over the comics, you will be bored to tears. Don't imagine that all that physique is going to make him the great lover. I know that type. He will probably go at you like a bull in a china shop, as a change from weight-lifting.'

But Mary went out with this hulk of manhood for nearly a year, until in fact he was put in charge of the digging operations outside the house of some lord or other near Park Lane. According to Bill, he was a 'real toff', graciously condescending to say good morning to him, and remarking how well and quickly Bill's men were getting on with the job. We were both getting bored to tears with all this talk of 'his lordship'—it had progressed to that by now—when one evening we were astounded to hear that Bill was giving this lord lessons in weight-lifting.

At first neither Mary nor I realized the implications of this; people had purer minds in those days. But the next thing we heard was that Bill was giving up being just a simple son of the soil. This lord was giving him an education, new clothes, even having him taught to drive and installing him in a luxury flat. Even we could see what that meant.

As this was about my last evening in Los Angeles I decided to telephone Albert. I waited until midnight, about eight o'clock in England. I heard his voice even more clearly than when I telephone him from London. In fact, I was sorry that I told him I could hear every word, because Albert said, 'Are you missing me? Are you homesick?'

To be honest I was neither; I was having far too good a time and enjoying America. Still, Albert is very long-suffering and doesn't mind, really, so long as I'm happy. Well, he has to live with me, so it's best to keep me happy.

I was to have a change of escort in this city. Michael was coming out and Toby would go back to England. I was not too worried about this change; in fact to be honest I rather welcomed it for Toby's sake, as I think that he had had enough. I had by now got used to him and understood that his silence didn't mean he was bored, merely that he was not there. With Michael I should be able to say what *I* wanted to do, *and* do it. Furthermore, he wouldn't know any more than I did how to get around. He had never been to America, so he wouldn't be any more confident than I was. Perhaps, too, he wouldn't know the best places to go and dine, as Toby did. I really had enjoyed all the different restaurants where we had dinner. I had even acquired a lot more confidence in ordering than I had before I came to America.

Just before Michael arrived I heard the news that Governor Wallace had been shot. Who would want to be a politician here?

Before Toby left, we all went out to dinner; it was very pleasant to be taken out by two escorts. At least, I thought so at first. But when, endeavouring to provide some intelligent conversation, I said to Michael, 'What do you think of Governor Wallace being shot?' he just laconically replied, 'Yes, I heard. So what?' and he and Toby went back to talking agents' business as though *that* was a matter of life and death.

Still, on this last evening Toby was charming. I wondered if it were because he was getting away. Or perhaps I didn't appreciate him enough. If he was never wildly enthusiastic, neither was he ever aggressive. In fact we had had only one real disagreement since we left England, which just shows what angelic dispositions we both have. Too late I began to look at him with some regret; perhaps Michael would not be as easy as I thought. After all, we had only met on some half-dozen occasions. All I knew of him was that he was excessively polite and always ready to fall in with anything that I wanted to do. These would be admirable traits out here—if he still had them out here. Probably he would not be nearly so efficient as Toby when it came to retrieving our luggage at the airports, or trying to get a taxi. Still, he might even breakfast with me. If there is anything that I like, it is having somebody to talk to at the breakfast-table. Little did I foresee that Michael would turn out to be just as bad-tempered as Toby, the only difference being that Michael did put in an appearance, but always brought a book with him and never raised his head from the page except to eat.

Later on in my room, I watched the news on television. There were realistic pictures of Governor Wallace talking to the crowd; one could even see the assassin. At breakfast the next morning it was the one topic of conversation. An American from Chicago was proclaiming in a loud voice that now there would be another outcry to do away with handguns. But in Chicago you weren't safe unless you had a gun, and if you outlawed guns, then only outlaws would have guns. Furthermore, if people wanted to murder and there were no guns, they would use a knife or some other weapon equally deadly. He may have been right. As I don't live there I don't know the conditions under which ordinary people live. In any case, I was so taken by surprise at having the company of both Toby and Michael for breakfast that I was unable to talk to anyone else. Even though I knew that the real reason they were there was that we all had to make an early start, I pretended to believe it was a treat for me on my last morning in Los Angeles—that's what they told me.

Somewhat to my surprise, I felt quite sad when Toby had gone, but I knew that the feeling wouldn't last—fortunately.

In the taxi to our airport, Michael was very solicitous, before we had even left the ground. I hoped he was not going to overdo the politeness and chivalry—which would soon become a bore.

I looked at the billboards along the road, all using beautiful girls to advertise different products—so persuasively that you really felt that by using some product or other you could look as beautiful. The fact that you were already years older in no way diminished your belief.

8: San Francisco

As I had foreseen, travelling with Michael was very different from travelling with Toby. On the plane to San Francisco I certainly got many sympathetic enquiries as to whether I was all right, or needed anything, but as this was the ninth plane journey I had made since leaving England I was no longer so apprehensive, even if I still didn't actually enjoy flying. On the other hand, when we landed at the airport, Michael wasn't anything like as quick and efficient as Toby had been. He did ask whether I could carry my heavy case. What he intended to do about it if I couldn't manage I don't know, for as he had burdened himself with enough luggage for three months instead of three weeks, it was perfectly obvious that he couldn't carry mine. Toby at least was honest in not even bothering to ask me if I could manage.

Our hotel was on Post Street, not far away from the city centre. When I saw it, I was struck by the radical change in the accommodation, now that Toby was no longer with me. All the hotels that he and I had stayed at were large and luxurious, with every amenity. This hotel was definitely just a place to sleep in, with no bars, lounges or shops, and there appeared to be a staff of only two. When I pointed out this come-down to Michael he immediately became highly indignant, saying irately, 'Why should we have to rough it? Let's change to a better hotel.'

But I would not. If Toby thought this would do well enough for us, then well enough it would have to be; besides, I like being a martyr at times.

Our rooms were on the top floor and I hastily located the stairs in case I needed to make a speedy exit. I was thinking of earth-quakes. Back home in England I had read an article which pointed out the imminence of such an event, and how all the people in San Francisco seemed not to worry about the prospect. I remembered thinking what an interesting article, never dreaming that one day I too would be in San Francisco. It was more than interest I felt now, especially as on the plane I was reading the *San Francisco Chronicle* in which a schools' superintendent warned that forty-four of the city's schools would have to close within three years unless they were made earthquake-proof. All it needed to do this, it appeared, was some 200 million dollars. He added, 'I am generally an optimistic man, but I am not optimistic that the community will come across with that kind of money in the short time left to us.' Too right they won't, was my thought, and wasn't sorry that I had only five days to worry about earth-quakes—especially as I felt sure that this hotel would be one of the first to collapse. As it was, I felt the hotel vibrate several times, and I apprehensively mentioned this to half of the staff, only to be laconically told, 'You don't need to worry; it's just the traffic. It happens all the time.'

Talk about living dangerously!

I was also told that, if an earthquake should strike, I mustn't panic, but stand under a door frame. But what if the earth opened up under my feet?

Once we got settled in I began to wonder about Michael. Would he, like Toby, have no desire to travel around on a coach tour? On my suggesting a trip around San Francisco to him, he cheerfully replied, 'Yes, Margaret, I'd love to go with you, but as we have only just arrived, I have several things to sort out.'

I actually believed this excuse at the time, not knowing that Michael was highly experienced in the art of getting out of any-thing he didn't want to do.

However, I was determined to see the sights; I knew that I would find someone to talk to on the coach, as indeed I did.

Our driver told us that the city is very proud of its civic centre, an attractive building with a dome somewhat like the Capitol in Washington. I notice in England they are now calling our ad-ministrative buildings civic centres instead of town halls.

We went also to the Mission Dolores which originally was a

Spanish mission built about 1780. It once had shops, stables and horses, but now there is just the church and the garden. Over five thousand Indians are buried in the churchyard. One of the bus passengers asked the driver what they died of; and he answered, 'The same thing that they are dying of now. Hunger, cold, disease and most of all, loss of self-respect.' A very uneasy silence followed this pronouncement, and one woman whispered to another, 'I bet he is half-Indian himself.'

We finally drove over Oakland Bay Bridge, eight miles long, the longest bridge in the world. In a way it's really two bridges, for about halfway it goes through an island. Coming back through this island and emerging from the tunnel you get a clear view of San Francisco, with sky-scrapers and houses on hills that seem to rise straight from the ocean. It was rather like a picture-postcard view and I remarked on this to the elderly man sitting next to me. He had not uttered a word until I spoke to him, but now he suddenly remarked, 'What do you know about bees?'

I hadn't a clue what he meant, I couldn't believe that he meant real bees. Perhaps he had said '*the* Bees'. This might be the name of an American baseball or ice-hockey team, or some other great all-American institution unknown to me, after the style of our Oddfellows or Buffaloes.

'What bees?' I asked him.

'What bees? Why, bees that make honey, of course.'

Now what is there about me that could make anybody imagine that I should be interested in bees? As a matter of fact I'm dead-scared of them; all that buzz-buzz makes me feel that any minute they are going to take a violent dislike to me. It's not a hobby I could ever take up. Wearing a hat like a straw roof heavily enmeshed in veiling doesn't add to one's personal attractions—though it must be something to be a queen bee and have all those males after you. Just imagine being lucky enough to have a selection!

Much to my annoyance, as I wanted to look at the scenery, he went on, 'My old daddy kept the finest bees in Milwaukee'—or he might have said Missouri for all I know—'my old daddy sold his honey for miles around; all the folks said it was the finest honey you could buy.'

Then this garrulous man continued to tell me the art of bee-keeping from A to Z—just how they swarm and how his old daddy could control the bees' desire to swarm, though with some types of bees the natural impulse couldn't be frustrated.

Yes, I thought, and that doesn't only apply to bees. Not with some types I've met anyway.

'My old daddy never got stung by his bees. He always said they only sting you if you are scared of them.'

'How does a bee know if you are afraid of it?'

'They can smell it, just like any hound-dog can.'

I found this statement very hard to believe, and I wished him and his old daddy to perdition.

In desperation, trying to change the subject, I rushed in with, 'Your father must have died some time ago surely?' After all, this man must have been getting on for seventy.

'He lived to be a hundred and three and all the folks for miles around came to his funeral,' including the bees I bet.

It would be my fate to sit next to this eccentric old man. If Michael had come it couldn't have happened. I mentally chalked up another black mark against him. When I told him that I now had added how to keep bees to the list of my accomplishments, he was quite impressed. At least, I think he was. It was a bit difficult to tell as he appeared to have slept all the afternoon and had only just woken up.

The next hour was devoted to sorting out where we should dine. Little did I know at this time that this was to be an evening ritual as Michael, unlike Toby, seemed to have not the faintest idea what would, or would not, be a good restaurant. We would start by having a couple of drinks in a bar, and this was always very enjoyable. I don't think that I have ever seen a city with so many bars. They were of all types, Irish, Scottish, some very opulent, others more like spit and sawdust. When we left the bar we'd try to find the restaurant that Michael had chosen. It was always, according to him, just down, or up, the road, but in actual fact it was streets away. Often, when we finally found it, he wouldn't like the look of it so we'd walk around some more. Some evenings I would have thankfully settled for a Joe Lyons. Michael said it was the time that elapsed between the drinks that annoyed me, but that's a calumny.

We had heard that a place called Fisherman's Wharf had

several good restaurants; we decided to try one there. Fisherman's Wharf was somewhat like a fishing village with all the boats moored in the lagoon, and nets draped around. Numerous stalls were selling the freshly-caught crabs and shrimp. There is also the last Cape Horn square-rigger moored there, a beautiful and graceful ship, but we didn't go on it. I'd had my share of exploring boats in Boston.

We had dinner at the Franciscan Sea-food Restaurant overlooking the Bay. The view was really wonderful; in fact, they say that only their food is better than the view from the huge dining-room windows; one can see right across the Bay to the far shore.

Before selecting from the menu I wanted to work out just what the items cost; but not Michael. He ordered with complete abandon and a total disregard of eventual settling-up. I found, as we travelled around, that he always did this—owing to being brought up in the lap of luxury, I suppose.

I ate delicious clams and, remembering my first dinner in Boston, this time I was very sparing with the horse-radish. This was followed by a perfect broiled sea-bream, a fish that I had not tasted since I used to cook them in domestic service.

When we left, the lamps were on all over the city, and its two bridges, strung with lights, looked as though they were suspended in space.

Just before I went to sleep I looked through my window and thought how night does change the face of a city.

Already I was falling in love with San Francisco. For one thing, there were pedestrians—not people who were out to get from one place to another in the shortest possible time, but people who strolled leisurely around looking into shop-windows.

San Francisco is built on seven hills, of which the most exclusive residential area is Nob Hill. When I told my mother this she immediately rushed in with, 'Fancy you going up there! How lucky you are! I know all about that place. It's where George Raft, who was born on the wrong side of the tracks—whatever that means—was always trying to get, so that he could marry the aristocratic and rich girl that he loved. But when he "made it" he found that it was his childhood sweetheart that he really loved.' Honestly, I believe my mum could write a film script herself, for now that she is old she seems to have become an incurable romantic, believing that love conquers all, and all that gush.

Most of the streets are so steep that the cars have to park crosswise into the kerbs. When I first got into a taxi driving down one of those streets, I felt as though I would fall on top of the driver. You swoop down the steep slope and then, where another street crosses, you flatten out, then repeat the process all over again.

The first morning I wandered around on my own, the best way really because you do not have to talk, just let everything soak in. People seemed so well dressed, and so friendly here. The sun was shining and I strolled along Union Street looking into the fascinating shops. It is full of little boutiques, art galleries and fine antiques interspersed with groups of interesting nineteenth-century houses. As I was gazing at these, a lady spoke to me, 'You don't live here, do you? I'm sure of it because you are wearing a summer dress. We know that it shouldn't be warm enough this time of the year so we are sweltering in suits. How sensible you are.'

It was almost impossible to lose myself, the streets were so well laid-out and sign-posted. I wandered happily up one street and down the next. To think that I was actually in San Francisco—I had been told never to call it Frisco.

More and more, as I visited places that previously I had only read about, I came to feel entirely divorced from England and everything appertaining to my life back there. It was as though time was suspended, a non-happening; I lost all sense of its passing. The reason was, I think, that never before had I had day after day with no work at all to do. Here there was absolutely nobody depending on any efforts of mine to help them. I didn't need to shop, cook meals or make beds. All was for my pleasure, my imagination. I just let it all sink in and I became rejuvenated.

Michael had not long breakfasted when I got back to the hotel. How could he waste time lolling around in bed when there was so much to see and do? It was not as though, like Toby, he had seen it all before; all this was as strange to him as to me, for which heaven be praised as I could openly express my astonishment at all we were seeing. His excuse was that he had been on the telephone, making arrangements for my future benefit. So much time was taken up on the telephone by both Toby and

Michael making arrangements for my future benefit that I was surely entitled to think that every place I visited would have the red carpet down and a brass band to welcome me. But I could not discover what all these arrangements consisted of, as everybody, in America at any rate, was completely unaware of my existence.

However, all this arduous work having given him a thirst—though he never needs any encouragement in that way, always dashing into a bar at the first opportunity—Michael suggested us walking until we found a pleasant bar; I knew it would be a short walk. We went into an Irish bar, and after Michael had sufficiently mellowed, he got into conversation with an American lady who lived in San Francisco. She was very friendly and welcoming and offered to drive us around the city; so we arranged to lunch at the Fairmont Crown, which is the cocktail bar of the Fairmont Hotel, twenty-nine storeys high. The hotel had the most opulent lobby that I had seen so far, with what seemed like miles of corridors and carpeting, chandeliers by the dozen, oil-paintings and mirrors: I felt as though I were entering the Palace of Versailles.

But it was in this hotel that I had another terrifying experience without any warning. I stepped casually into the lift, persuading myself that twenty-nine storeys wasn't all that high. But when I got inside and the doors had shut, I found that it was a glass-sided lift and went up on the outside of the building. Just fancy, crawling up twenty-nine storeys on the outside of the wall; I nearly fainted with the shock. The other people seemed to think that getting to the Crown Room in this way was great fun. They were uttering Oohs and Aahs at the marvellous view of the Golden Gate Bridge and the Bay. A notice in the lift said that this hair-raising ride took one minute, forty seconds; to me it seemed an eternity. I felt a great surge of sympathy for those men who stand on frail platforms painting the outside of extremely high buildings.

Our lady friend's car was one of those enormous American cars that are about three times as large as they need to be. There are hundreds of these on the roads taking up a lot of space, and most of them seem to have only one person in them. She drove us around the Golden Gate Park. San Francisco claims that this is the largest man-made park in the world, over 1,000 acres and three and a half miles long, half a mile wide. It is a very beautiful place, and it certainly says much for the ingenuity of the man who conceived it, a Scotsman, John McLaren. Everything is so well arranged that it gives the impression of having been there since time immemorial; yet a hundred years ago it was just sand-dunes. There are attractions for everybody—lovely gardens, paths for horse-riding, a lake for the children, aquarium and planetarium. It even has a Dutch windmill that at one time supplied the water. There is also a charming replica of a Japanese tea-garden, beautifully laid out, not in the least synthetic or commercial.

Each American state seemed to have its own state park, and these are so designed that the natural beauty has been left unspoilt. The state parks are not like town parks in England, which are obviously man-made. Partly I suppose because there are no amenities to start with. In America the parks are made around what was already there, lakes, waterfalls, rocks and trees. They are looked after, and kept in the original pattern of nature, and they always seem to cover miles of land. The immensity of America is something that I still cannot grasp. The land goes on, mile after mile, never-ending, and every kind of climate and temperature can be found there. My Texan friend told me that his state alone is bigger than the whole of the continent of Europe.

It was very pleasant to drive around San Francisco with somebody who knew it so well. I wanted to keep it all in my memory so I left the conversation to Michael and our lady friend; they seemed to have a lot in common as the talking was non-stop. He said that he was just being polite; somebody had to answer her. This unaccustomed effort of his, resulted in complete exhaustion. By the time we got back to our hotel Michael was fit for nothing but immediate retirement to his bed for at least a couple of hours.

'What shall I do, then?' I enquired.

'Anything you like so long as you don't need me to do it with,' was all the answer I got.

So, for no reason at all, I decided to have a sauna bath, never in my life having had this experience. During my walk around I had noticed several of these establishments, though, judging by the advertisements on the outside, they seemed more for a few hours' amusement than for their original purpose; perhaps the end results were the same. The one I chose said, 'Massage by five lovely girls'—not all at once surely—'come in and meet Pansy, Pearl and Sapphire'. I forget the other names. I couldn't find a sign that advertised, 'Massage by five lovely men', otherwise I might have chosen that one; I shall have to get Women's Lib on to it.

I found that if I didn't want to disrobe completely, and I didn't, I could leave on just the minimum. Twenty years ago I would probably have flung everything off with gay abandon; but that's another story. I was given an enormous towel to wrap myself in and taken to a room that had stone benches. I lay down on one and tried to see through the steam if there was anybody other than me; I was the one and only. I couldn't tell how the steam came out, but after about ten minutes I began to perspire profusely; in fact I got so hot that I began to get alarmed at being shut up and nearly baking. However, before I completely melted away I was taken to another room and given a cold shower; this was very invigorating.

Sauna baths are supposed to rid you of impurities (physical, not moral). I can't say that I felt ten years younger and fit for anything, but there you are: I didn't expect a miracle.

When it was all over and I was drinking a cup of coffee, the proprietor came over and introduced himself as Raphael, with the accent on the last two syllables. He found that my home was Brighton and became quite excited, saying that he had lived there, just by the railway, for three years.

In fact, Raphael was as English as me; he had been in America only five years, and his real name was Ralph.

'My dear, you don't want to drink that stuff, do you? Wouldn't you like something stronger? What about a gin and tonic? And let's have a little chat about Brighton. I do miss it.'

Never being averse to a free drink, even at four in the afternoon, I agreed that it would be a good idea.

Raphael had a very grand flat right at the top of the building; well, *he* was obviously proud of it but I thought that his taste in décor was somewhat bizarre—walls covered with black paper; an orange frieze; settee and chairs in tangerine velvet; and cushions of the same colour all over the floor on the black carpet. There were pictures hanging on the wall that left absolutely nothing to the imagination. Chosen by Leon I was told. I tried to imagine him and decided that he must be somewhat decadent. Still, by the time that I had had a few gins, the décor became far less overwhelming, especially as I was entertained by a collection of hilarious stories about the art of running a sauna establishment. I protested that such things couldn't happen in England, but Raphael assured me that where he worked in Brighton was just as bad—or good.

Raphael had a very wealthy and very obese woman client, who came along every week to be slapped and pummelled in a vain effort to reduce the mountain of flesh. 'My dear,' whispered Ralph, 'you've no idea how I suffered, for she insisted on me working on her; until I took on Leon, that is. Now she prefers him, for which heaven be thanked. It used to take me most of the next day to recover my strength.'

Looking at his willowy figure I thought there wasn't much to recover at any time.

'As it is,' Ralph went on, 'Leon asks me for extra money after every session with her—not that I blame him. But she is one of the hazards of this game. The young and shapely don't need us, or if they do, certainly don't expect to pay. Believe me, Margaret' —we had progressed to first names by now—'it's not all honey. Honestly, darling, until I had made enough money to employ others to do the hard work I was always so tired that I wasn't much good to anybody.'

He didn't specify what sex he was no good to; perhaps he was ambidextrous. As he shared the flat with Leon he probably shared other things also.

Just then Leon came in to see what all the laughter was about. What a handsome man he was, with dark curly hair, flashing eyes and a very attractive physique. Not that I have ever gone to town over these very handsome men, finding, so to speak, that the good looks are all and only—when you have that you have the entire man. Because he is so handsome he hasn't had to bother about other accomplishments. I very well remember Jack Harper, a young man I met when I was nineteen, and nineteen then was equal to about fourteen today as far as sophistication is concerned. As I was a cook by this age I had more free time, dashing out to meet this Jack every evening from nine to ten as well as in my official time off. He professed great affection for me every time we met, but I suffered agonies of jealousy, wondering what he was doing when I wasn't with him. I felt that they should have invented chastity belts for men. Jack was so charming to be with, kissing with enough warmth to make me feel he loved me, but not so much that I had to be apprehensive of the next move. The ending of this romance was such a shock that I have never forgotten it. We went to a friend's engagement party, about twenty-five young people. Some of the girls were very pretty, too. All went well for a couple of hours, when suddenly my Jack disappeared, as did one of these unattached pretty girls. Needless to say, I wasn't one to suffer without taking some action, so I searched the garden. Eventually I looked into the bedroom where we had left our coats, and there was Jack with a girl. It wasn't so much that they were making love, though that would have been bad enough, it was the way that they were doing it that simply petrified me; I couldn't believe what I saw or that people did such things. Still, in a way, it was a relief to lose him and be able to drop out of the competition.

Leon was about thirty-five, a mixture of a Spanish mother and Irish father, though where they were now he had no idea. At the age of fourteen he had left home, such as it was, to look after himself. He seemed to have done everything, from being a procurer and pimp; spending a year travelling with a wealthy elderly lady as a sort of bodyguard; smuggling brandy; and running a gambling joint. 'But never have I had anything to do with drugs,' Leon said, as though that excused all the other offences.

Both Raphael and Leon urged me on to talk about my life, but even I had the sense to see that sitting in this somewhat decadent-looking room with two men lolling on the floor, and being in another country, was hardly the ideal setting for a cosy chat. I was inwardly amazed at finding myself there; neither Toby nor Michael had promised me such exciting adventures. Mind you, it cost me quite a few dollars, but then it's seldom that one gets something for nothing, especially experience, and it was a lot more exciting than book research.

Michael was somewhat sceptical when I told him I'd had a girl masseuse at the sauna, but he didn't know me very well then.

Strolling around in this city was fun. There was so much to see within walking distance. The contrast was all the more noticeable as I had so recently left Los Angeles. I walked along Union Street again. Once it was a street of almost Victorian-type houses, and it's still possible to visualize how it originally looked.

Most of the lovely things in the shops were an astronomical price, though they all took credit cards. This credit-card system is an open sesame to buying an Aladdin's treasure, unless one exercises severe restraint and thinks about the eventual settling-day. It's so easy and tempting to enter the shops, knowing that one hasn't to produce real money, just a small piece of apparently worthless plastic. One wouldn't even think of the transaction in the ordinary way, but when all one has to do is to show a card, it's just as though one were being given a lovely present. Every day is a birthday. I found out even more about how easy it is to become a 'big spender'. Michael and I went to a play called *The Committee*. There were six men and two women who did satirical sketches on political and topical subjects. They were very witty and clever. One of these sketches was about credit cards and how you first obtain one: it's easy: just fill in all the credit-card applications that there are, however obscure the company. You are bound to receive a favourable reply from at least one of them. Once you can say that you already have a card, the rest will follow suit; they won't want to be left out of the deal. And if, this sketch proposed, you knew what to do, you could postpone payment indefinitely. Inform the San Francisco branch that your forwarding address is New York; in New York your forwarding address is Paris. From Paris you can have a forwarding address to anywhere else in the world. It would take years before your forwarding came full circle.

Towards the end of the show there was a bit too much audience participation for me. Primarily, I go to the theatre to relax and be entertained, not to help the actors do their job. Besides, audience participation generally means that the ones who join in have gone there specially for that purpose. They are convinced that they can do as well as, if not better than, the actors on the stage. This is their chance to prove it.

Michael liked that part of the play. But then he is young and it's the done thing to be in this kind of Round House confrontation.

Michael, with rare decisiveness, had said that we were going to dine in a Japanese restaurant. I had never eaten Japanese food, but I had seen pictures in magazines where everybody sat on cushions on the floor eating off low tables. It looked very oriental and adventurous, but I couldn't see myself stretched out on the floor to eat. Thinking about the difficulty of rising gracefully would worry me all the evening. So I insisted it would have to be a restaurant with proper chairs and tables. The one that we chose specialized in *teppan-yaki* style of cooking—whatever that is supposed to mean. We sat down at a long table and I found it somewhat disconcerting to find six other people already sitting there. In addition, the centre of the tables appeared to be a large, flat-topped steel kitchen range.

A Japanese chef came out, tipped food on to the ferociously hot steel top, and right before our very eyes he proceeded to chop and slice like mad—meat, vegetables, enormous shrimps. Having all this prepared in front of us was a great breaker-down of inhibitions; before long we eight were no strangers to each other. Of course, the sight of me trying to consume my food with only two long pointed sticks was a source of hilarity to those who were manipulating these things with great dexterity. That included Michael, and I suspect that this was the reason he refused to ask for proper cutlery; he said it wasn't the done thing in a restaurant like this. I think my lack of skill just made him feel superior; so far he had had very few opportunities to feel that way. Nevertheless, although every piece of food I tried to dip into the delicious sauces just fell in, and Michael's whole attention was devoted to the pretty kimono-clad girls who were serving, I managed to enjoy the meal.

People were very friendly in San Francisco. On the only occasion that I did lose my way, a very pleasant lady went out of her way to set me right, and in spite of my propensity for plain speaking, only two people answered rudely, one of those being a taxi-driver.

It's as well that one can so easily walk around in San Francisco because the taxis seem to cost an awful lot of money for a short ride. I remarked on this to my cab-driver, who looked a nice amiable young man, and he said, 'Ma'am, if you had to drive up and down these streets like being on a scenic railway you'd charge a lot too. I can wear out a cab quicker than you can wear out your shoes.'

He asked me what I was doing in San Francisco. When I told him that I was collecting impressions to write a book he said, 'Go out to Berkeley University; you'll get plenty of impressions from the kids out there. You can't criticize us until you have talked to the young people.'

'What makes you think that I am going to criticize?'

'Well, you can't write a book without. But just remember that living in America isn't living as you know it in England. The British come over here and assume that, because we speak English, we are the same as them, and all the time they are here they are comparing our way of life with theirs. Here we don't love our country, we love our state. What you don't realize is that most of our states are larger than your entire British Isles.'

All this was said in the nicest possible way—mind you, I still had to pay the fare. He told me that he hoped to earn enough money to hitch-hike to England next year.

'How long are you reckoning on staying there?' I asked.

'Oh, in England, just two weeks. I reckon I'll have seen all of it in that time. Then I'll cross the Channel to France and Holland.'

Honestly, where do these Americans get their idea of the size of England?

'Do you mind?' I asked him. 'We are not as small as that. You can't hitch-hike all over England in two weeks. You must be thinking of the Isle of Wight, not our island. For one thing, we don't rush about as fast as everyone does over here. Certainly you could pay a lightning visit to our main cities, but there are hundreds of places in England that are worth seeing. Even I haven't seen them all yet. Just because we are that microscopic pink bit on your map, don't get the wrong idea. Everything's closer together, that's all.'

We parted with mutual expressions of goodwill, and we may meet in Brighton.

More and more I was charmed by this city. Perhaps it was something to do with the weather. I was warned of the proverbial fog, that for days one can see nothing, but so far all was warmth and sunshine. Everyone was friendly, no one made you feel you were an intruder; the streets were clean and colourful. Even in a huge store, like Macy's, I enjoyed my shopping. I bought a dress and the young girl who served me went to endless trouble, explaining the American sizes and how much in English money it would cost. She was a university student, working in this store to pay for next year's tuition. She had just completed her freshman year—the first year. When I asked her what she was studying she said, 'I'm writing a book on the history of puzzles. In particular Chinese ones.' I didn't like to pass an adverse comment, but I wouldn't have thought that there was much of a future in that. What do you take up when leaving university? Surely, even in America, there can't be many jobs where a knowledge of Chinese puzzles is an asset. Unless, of course, this knowledge leads to elucidating the enigma of the Chinese mentality.

After the conversation with my nice taxi-driver and talking to the student in Macy's, I tried to convince Michael that a visit to Berkeley University was a must. He needed no convincing that for me it was a must, saying hypocritically, 'Yes, Margaret, but you will enjoy it far more on your own, talking to all those charming young men; you don't want me there too.'

What can you say to a person like that?

My heart sank when I first saw our coach-driver, a Mr Pinkson, as I could tell that he was going to be one of those life-and-soul-of-the-party types. In actual fact he was so good-humoured that one couldn't mind his being a bit overwhelming. He sang the song, 'I left my heart in San Francisco' as we went over Oakland Bridge. His voice was considerably more melodious than mine—not that that means much.

Although Berkeley is only one of the nine campuses of the University of California, it is a huge place. Even going round it in the coach took some time. There are so many different buildings devoted to every subject under the sun—perhaps even Chinese puzzles? Grass and trees abounded. It seemed a very pleasant place to work and sleep.

The new Museum of Art had only recently been opened, but already somebody had scrawled across it, 'Art is to be found in the streets.' In my opinion it certainly wasn't to be found in the outside of that building, which seemed singularly divorced from art.

The Berkeley students had, during the previous three days, rioted and protested over President Nixon's escalation of the war in Vietnam. They had smashed many shop-windows and over-turned cars. These actions seemed somewhat incongruous when taken in conjunction with the banners they carried proclaiming, 'Let us live in peace. No more war.' Smashing and looting are hardly peaceful pursuits.

We were told by our singing driver that we could walk around the campus for forty-five minutes. Some of the passengers were too nervous to do this, in view of the militancy there. But trusting to my age and luck, I immediately walked on the campus, and enjoyed myself immensely. My so-called cockney voice was a great success here, as was the information about how I had acquired a late education. The students thought I was marvellous; how nice it is to be praised! I had received precious little of this from my escorts.

Naturally, I asked about the recent riots, and two of the students, Mike and Rick, complained bitterly about the militant and aggressive minority. 'There are seventy thousand students,' said Mike, 'and about five thousand who cause trouble. But they are the ones who get all the publicity. California University used to be the best in America, if not the best in the world. But now, because of these riots we attract the radicals and the Left; the type that we want won't come here because they feel that their studies will be interrupted.'

Both Mike and Rick were doing seven years in Berkeley. They told me that it costs about 11,000 dollars a year; that includes lodging, food, books and other things.

Rick said, 'I borrow every year from the bank to supplement my grant; I reckon by the time I leave here I'll owe about five thousand dollars.'

I expressed surprise that the banks would loan money without security. After all, he might not pass, so how could he pay back the money in that case?

'The federal government guarantees the money to the bank. But we have to attend the lectures, and our cards have to be marked to show that we have. Anyway, I shall pass, and work here. My starting salary will be four hundred pounds, not dollars, per month.'

I asked another student, an extremely randy-looking young man, what he did in his leisure time. He asked me if I wanted a practical demonstration; somewhat regretfully I told him not to bother.

'Well, ma'am,' he said, in a very sexy voice, 'as I haven't much money—and although America is supposed to be the land of the free, there's not much you can get without money—I pass the time strolling on the sidewalks, stepping over all the dog-mess that is lying there from the pampered pets of the high society living in Berkeley. They're the only things pampered here, I can assure you.'

'What's that tower over there?'

'That's the Campanile, for would-be suicides. Most of them come down the same way they went up. We call it our Freudian phallic symbol. God knows there's plenty of vital urges around here.'

As by this time he was holding my hand and I could tell the conversation was going to be somewhat bawdy, I hurriedly departed, saying that I had to get back to the coach. As I walked back over the campus I was surprised by the amount of rubbish lying about. I was told that the janitors were on strike. The students couldn't clean up because that would make them blacklegs; besides the janitors weren't paid enough.

Just outside the campus was a collection of what appeared to be the rejects of society, or perhaps *they* had rejected *it*. They were dressed in a mat of hair and beards, ragged jeans and patches. One of them was wearing a vest with 'Jesus loves me' written across it. If so, He was probably the only one who did, as the drop-out looked so repulsive that even a mother would find it impossible to love him. Another, almost as peculiar, was selling cakes. 'Uncapitalistic, edible cookies' was written on his board. I was hungry, but I decided to wait until I could buy a few capitalistic but germ-free cookies.

All down University Avenue were hitch-hikers holding up boards showing where they wanted a lift to—Oregon, Detroit, East and West. One hopeful had Hawaii on his board.

Our coach had only just started on the return journey when a large red lorry ran into us. Nobody was hurt, but the front of the coach was severely dented. Our driver and the lorry-driver got out and had what appeared to be a furious altercation on the sidewalk. Most of the passengers, with that instinct that prevails the world over for not wanting to get mixed up with the police, began to tell each other that they hadn't seen whose fault it was. Everybody became exceedingly friendly while they synchronized their stories. *I* had seen that it was the fault of the lorry-driver; he went over a double line. I too hoped not to have to give an opinion; after all self-preservation comes first. Besides I didn't want to get involved in anything so soon after Michael took over. Probably he would think it was my fault; even if he didn't, he was sure to blame me. But then I had already found that whatever went amiss on this American tour was my fault.

When Mr Pinkson got back in the coach, however, all had been settled amicably, but we would have to wait half an hour for another coach. This was a golden opportunity for Mr Pinkson to tell a variety of funny stories. He worked hard but nobody laughed; it really was a shame. I think that he breathed a sigh of relief when our coach arrived. I bet that he told his wife this coach-load was a dead loss.

On the way back we stopped at the Mormon Temple. This was an enormous edifice topped with a tall golden spire in the middle of four smaller golden spires. There were bay-trees specially imported from Greece, four full-time gardeners for the extensive grounds, the whole thing costing five million dollars. Frankly I was horrified. I could not see what all this had to do with such a simple act as worshipping their God, or indeed any God. They pray continually for the living and the dead, from 6 a.m. to 10 p.m.—after that you've had it. I was surprised to be told that they have baptisms for the dead.

'Suppose the departed doesn't want to be baptized. After all, as he didn't bother or want to while he was alive, presumably he cares even less now. Isn't it cheek of his relations to do something over his dead body?'

'They can reject it in the spirit world if they want to,' was the answer. I never imagined that even when you have departed this life you still have to make decisions. No rest anywhere it seems!

The baptismal font rested on the backs of twelve life-sized oxen covered with gold leaf. These represent the twelve tribes of Israel. I left this ornate and expensive edifice with a feeling of depression at the thought of so much money spent on the trappings of religion.

I think that our driver must have at some time driven the American equivalent of a char-à-banc, for on the way back he was urging us to join him in a song, 'Roll out the Barrel'. What a hope with this lot! The majority verdict on poor Mr Pinkson was that he was 'too familiar'. So, getting no response, he switched to facts and figures, such as how many insurance companies there were in San Francisco (nearly 700); highest building 41 storeys). Out came the notebooks and all this was jotted down, though what earthly use it was to anybody I don't know.

I really do believe that Michael, during my absence, had begun to feel rather conscience-stricken at thus pushing me off on my own. He needn't have worried. I had already realized that, as soon as I left England, chivalry was a dead duck. However, there was Michael, waiting in the lobby of our hotel, and he immediately suggested going out for a drink, which is a remark I always like to hear. The drinking laws are a bit archaic in California. Nobody under twenty-one is allowed to drink, not even a glass of wine in a restaurant, and they are not allowed in the bars at any time.

We decided that a ride on the antiquated cable-cars was a must. If you cannot get a seat, it needs a lot of practice to remain in an upright position, as the cars sway about alarmingly and make loud clanking noises all the time. At the end of the journey the cars have to be turned around manually, and they provide a constant source of amusement to visitors with remarks like, 'You've heard of the topless; we are the brakeless.' It costs 25 cents however far you go, and that's good value for the whole journey. Women have only just been allowed to stand up on the outside—another victory for Women's Lib. Mind you, one trip on the trolley-car was enough for me—a less likely vehicle for romance I can't imagine. Yet I saw a film, years ago, that had Clark Gable for the hero; I forget the heroine, she was never important to me. In the film Clark Gable sat next to this girl, who was a complete stranger to him. First he put his arm round her to stop her swaying about, then he hummed a little romantic ditty, though how she ever heard it above the clanking and clatter of the cable-car was a mystery to me; I couldn't hear a word that Michael was saying; both he and Toby talk in such quiet voices that I have seriously contemplated buying an ear-trumpet. Not that it really matters if I miss half of what they say; it's generally about what *they* want me to do, and that seldom coincides with what *I* want to do. It's all to do with their upbringing. If, like me, they had been brought up with a pack of brothers and sisters, all living in three rooms, they too would have learnt to shout to get a hearing.

We went down to Chinatown in the evening, and walked down Grant Avenue, where some of the buildings had many-coloured balconies decorated with very ornate gilded carvings. The shops were full of strange-looking tins and herbs and lanterns were hanging outside. Some of the doors were painted with very bold brush strokes in black and gold and the roofs of the houses had upward-curling eaves.

Not so long ago my idea of Chinatown was a place of esoteric opium dens, with mysterious figures slinking in and out of half-hidden doorways, but the real Chinese quarter is nothing like that. We had dinner in a splendid oriental restaurant called The Empress of China. This Empress is a mythological one; she represents the Spirit of the Earth. We came straight out of the lift into a charming garden court, with banks of plants and flowers, a fountain, and the largest goldfish that I have ever seen—or perhaps they were carp. As for the décor of the restaurant itself, it was very ornate and grand. It had antique green and gold chandeliers, jade-green silk on the walls and peacock feathers. But what recommended it to me above all was that knives and forks were on the table as well as Chinese chopsticks. Reading all the information about the Empress of China, we learned that each dish was an epicurean triumph, cooked to perfection—treasured dishes of past dynasties and enticing favourites of the Dowager's Royal Household. In my opinion all this rhetoric was hardly justified by the food or service, though Michael consumed his choice as though it was a Lucullan banquet and obviously had decided that in this imitation palace food and conversation did not mix.

What few people there were in the restaurant were as solemn and dedicated as though they were either about to launch a new gastronomic era on the world, or preparing for the last rites. I am not fond of these establishments where one is made to feel a criminal if one laughs, and where a knowledge of good food is equal to winning an Olympic gold medal.

As for all the reams of print about cooking, there are as many books on the subject as there are on sex, perhaps because the pleasures of the former seem to lead to the pleasures of the latter —both pleasures being no longer simple. Nowadays, older couples, reading modern sex books, must suddenly discover that what they had previously considered enjoyable, couldn't possibly have been so. I should think that by the time they retire to bed and work out which of the fifty-seven varieties is best for them, it's too late anyway.

We dined in some very good restaurants in San Francisco, but when Michael found a lovely place for a quick snack, called Hippo Hamburgers, I'm sure that I found it equally enjoyable. It was beautifully clean with flowers on every table, smiling wait-resses and the best hamburgers I have ever tasted. They had about thirty-five to forty different kinds, from the 'Stripburger' which was served without extras, to the very elaborate 'Tahitian burger', served with a sweet-sour sauce, pineapple, grapes, chest-nut- and banana-fritters—laid on a 'Polynesian bed', but I don't know what that meant; I think Michael would have liked a Polynesian girl as an 'after'. One may be satirical about the Americans' 'burger mentality', but for an inexpensive and filling meal served in very clean surroundings, a hamburger takes a lot of beating.

This being my last complete day and night in San Francisco, I had an early breakfast, for I was determined to walk around and see as much of the city as possible, so that the happy memories would remain. Even without much money I don't think a visitor could be bored, there are so many things to see and do that cost nothing.

My home town of Brighton is hilly, but this city is literally all ups and downs like a scenic railway. After walking downhill in a series of jerky steps and then puffing up I did eventually get used to it. I walked all the way up Telegraph Hill, one of the famous hills of San Francisco. It has very attractive old-fashioned houses, where the artists live. I walked down Lombard Street, which the Americans say is the crookedest street in the world—though I don't know what proof they can have of that.

Even the sky-scrapers in this city are not really ugly. The façade is broken up with attractive bas-relief. A new Westbury Hotel is going up with half-bay windows to break the monotony of a flat building.

Not only is this city full of restaurants of every nationality under the sun, but also it seems full of churches of all denominations. I should think that every variety of religious belief is catered for; on one walk I counted fifteen different sects. I wandered into a small art gallery, full of pictures by young and unknown artists. One that I would have liked was a splendid view of the Golden Gate Bridge with the sun setting over it. I expect Michael would have thought it was corny but I do like a picture that has a definite subject; for one thing you know the right way up to hang it. I got into conversation with an American, like me a tourist, though he came only from Massachusetts. He explained to me some of the finer points of the paintings and why some cost so much more than others.

On hearing that I wanted to visit the history room of the Wells Fargo Bank, he said that he too would like to see it. Unfortunately, when we got there the bank was closed—perhaps the horses hadn't got through; though I believe that Wells Fargo do use more modern methods of transporting money and mail, and from the length of time it takes for some of my letters to reach me I reckon our post office has borrowed the horses.

To console ourselves, we decided to have a drink and get properly introduced to each other; a bar, as he and I agreed, was the best place for doing this. Over a vodka Collins he told me that his name was Sam Nelson; that he had been a widower for two years and was finding it one hell of a lonely time; there was no fun in doing things on your own. I asked him why he didn't marry again as America seemed to have no end of attractive widows. He became rather embarrassed at this; from what I could understand, his wife's death had been such a traumatic experience that he had not been able to perform since then. As there was nothing I wanted to do about that, I sympathetically said that it would probably pass, and we talked of other things. Sam told me that America was rapidly changing, and not for the better in his opinion, as materialistic values had taken the place of the good-neighbour policy. Or rather, America's one idea was now to be a good neighbour anywhere but in her own country. Americans had lost faith in their leaders and instead of the community spirit it was everyone for himself; money was the only passport to what they considered the good life. I said that money was desired by the English too, but Sam, whose only knowledge of England was a visit he and his wife made ten years ago, looked upon our country as an ideal place. No rush, no ugly skyscrapers, everybody so polite and friendly! He added, 'Though in our tour around I did see one thing that struck me as ironical. We are always being criticized for our ostracism of the Negroes, but in several of your pubs I saw notices which stated, "No gypsies served here". So you don't exactly have welcome on the mat for your aliens if their colour and way of life happen to be different.' With this I agreed.

Sam came from a place called Worcester, and thought his state of Massachusetts was the best state in America. He told me it was one of the original thirteen and the Pilgrim Fathers first settled there: no, none of them were his ancestors. The Institute of Technology was also the best in America. Here was yet another American who thought in terms of his state, rather than his country: all to do with the size, I'm sure.

By the time we had drunk the third Collins, Sam began to rhapsodize about his departed wife, so I decided it was time to depart too. It's not that I'm hard-hearted but I had had, in the past, one experience of widower's grief occasioned by alcohol, and that was too much. I could tell that Sam was getting ready to disclose intimate details of their life together. He had already got as far as, 'We were made for each other in every way,' when I interrupted—in as nice a way as possible—by saying I had to get back to my hotel; somebody was waiting for me.

Michael was somewhat impatiently waiting to go out to lunch, one of the few things that galvanizes him into any form of activity. After lunch we went again to Fisherman's Wharf. Although this is now a somewhat touristy place, nevertheless it's still worth a visit, with its boats and nets and dozens of little shops. Deciding to act like tourists, we went into Ripley's 'Believe it or not' museum, a place that I wouldn't cross the road to visit in the ordinary way. The museum is billed as 'interesting to all ages, from five to a hundred and five'—though I should think that a person of that age had seen enough oddities in a long life.

The cannibal curios were somewhat gruesome, though we were assured that cannibalism is dying out except for one tribe, who eat only departed relatives or the leader of the tribe. Many people in England have felt the same way about their relatives, and even more so about their leaders, whether Left or Right. But we only eat them metaphorically.

For our last evening here I discovered that Michael had, 'as a special treat', arranged a Bay Cruise. 'We simply must do it; everybody who visits San Francisco goes on a Bay Cruise at least once.' Although he had never been here before he liked to make these statements as though he knew all about it. I agreed, with some reservations, wondering if the water would be rough.

I can never understand why I, who am so strong physically and so level-headed, should have to suffer from what seem to be nervous complaints—vertigo, claustrophobia and seasickness. I should be able to overcome such weaknesses, especially the last. My last experience of being on the water I had no wish to recall, as it involved my being carried off on a stretcher from the boat at Newhaven. This somewhat unusual method of disembarkation was due to Albert and me having differing ideas of a cure for seasickness. Albert pins his faith on a tot or two of neat whisky and persuaded me to try this—not that I needed much persuading. Unfortunately, I had already put into effect my own method which was to swallow two pills guaranteed to keep seasickness away. The combination of these two cures was practically lethal. I went out like a light and knew no more until deposited on the quayside at Newhaven. I must admit it was a successful crossing of the Channel in that I was oblivious to the waves.

By the time that Michael and I arrived at the dockside, any eagerness for the trip had abated, especially after Michael related a few of his sailing experiences—greatly exaggerated I'm sure—in which he had crossed the Channel in a raging gale and was one of the few passengers brave enough to walk the decks. And of course, *he* was never seasick.

To me, this boat appeared to be rolling considerably, though Michael assured me that the water was like a mill-pond. Yes, just as it leaves the water-wheel, I thought. However, with customary disregard for my own comfort, I made up my mind to go on the boat. I could tell by Michael's keenness that this trip was for his benefit—not mine. So, endeavouring not to remember the *Titanic*, the *Mary Celeste* and ships that pass in the night, never to be seen again, I embarked on my treat. The particular cruise that we were on included champagne, and a dinner when we landed at Tiburon. I was sceptical whether this would add any-thing to the pleasure of the cruise, as my experience of anything that includes free champagne—admittedly not very extensive—is that at the best it tastes like sweet water, and at the worst like nothing on earth.

All kinds of people were on the Bay Cruise. Some of the ladies were wearing long dresses and jewels, as though they were about to dine at the captain's table on the *Queen Elizabeth*; others wore old jeans and sandals, obviously prepared to work their passage across.

There was supposed to be an interesting commentary on the points of interest, but if so the voice was lost in the prevailing din. Still, Michael was an absolute wizard at getting the cham-pagne; it was quite good too.

On the way we passed the island of Alcatraz, the federal peni-tentiary until it was closed in 1963. A couple of years ago the American Indian Nationalists took over the island as a symbol of their lost heritage! Needless to say, they very soon got ejected. There are plans to make it into a cultural centre; I don't see why the Indians couldn't have had the island for *their* cultural centre. Since Americans now have guilt feelings about their past treat-ment of the Indians, why not make a gesture to those that are left?

For the dinner, one had in theory a choice of five restaurants, but in fact I suspect that the food was much the same at all of them, as the advent of such a crowd of people all at one time would not make for selective meals. But it was very pleasant and the view of the two bridges strung with lights was entrancing.

Tiburon, where we landed, was a rather quaint waterside village; the harbour was full of large luxurious-looking yachts. Well, to me they seemed large. I would have liked to have seen Tiburon by daylight. The shops and little art galleries were very attractive, but they were, unfortunately, closed.

I left San Francisco next morning with great reluctance and a very real feeling of regret. In this city, I had felt far less of a stranger in a strange land than in any other city I had so far seen.

In a way, this leaving was entirely different; we were leaving not only San Francisco but the United States too, to go to Canada.

During the last war I met many Canadians; several regiments were stationed in Hove, in particular, the 4th Battalion of the British Columbia Regiment, from Vancouver—and we were on our way to Vancouver.

When I worked in the Canadians' officers canteen in Hove, I was continually being told, 'Do not confuse us with Americans. Just because we share a border does not mean we are alike; we are as different from Americans as chalk from cheese.' Never did I think the time would come when I could find out for myself.

9: Vancouver

I was in fact particularly pleased to be going to Vancouver because I have a nephew living there and he was meeting us at the airport. After nearly four weeks' absence from my home and family, it was really something to see somebody who 'belonged'. So many airports had I been through on this journey, so many people had I seen greeted affectionately, but never, up to now, had there been anybody waiting for me, prepared to make me feel welcome. It really was a happy feeling to see my nephew's smiling face waiting at the barrier.

The following day, Sunday, my nephew Nick collected me from the hotel to spend the day with him and his wife, who had just had a second baby. Michael could have come too but, as I very well knew, he had not the slightest desire to visit my relations. In fact, judging by the gleeful expression on his face as he saw me off, he was thanking his lucky stars that he had a whole day in which to do nothing. I have discovered that he can do nothing better than anybody I know, and get enthusiastic about it, too.

To save his wife having to cook, Nick took me to eat at a Swedish *smörgåsbord*, one of those places where a huge variety of food is set out on counters and you help yourself. For the one price you can keep coming back and refilling your plate. I discovered, too late, that the secret is to have just a little to start with, then you are still hungry enough to go around again and try the food you didn't take the first time; in fact, I saw one man go round three times; I shouldn't think there was much profit attached to a customer of that sort.

Vancouver seemed an exceedingly quiet and empty place, but Nick said this was because there was a long week-end holiday, the first after a very cold winter. Monday was an extra day's holiday for Queen Victoria's birthday; I forgot to ask which one. It does seem an anomaly that Canada should give a day off for her birthday while in England all her birthdays are ignored. After all, if anybody should think it an occasion for a celebration, it should be England; we had her for years, and the effects of her still linger on, not always beneficially either. Perhaps, now we have this craze for Victoriana, some patriotic person might get up a petition for the workers of England to unite and demand a public holiday in remembrance of that pillar of family life.

Nick assured me that our hotel, the Georgia, was one of the best in Vancouver. It was very luxurious and the food excellent, but the lounge bar as usual was dimly lit. Almost without exception in America the bars seemed to be the ultimate in gloom as far as lighting was concerned. I used to enter what at first appeared to be an underground cavern, it was so dark. After standing still for a while to get my bearings, faintly ahead I could see a bar. Groping my way towards it, I was always somewhat surprised to find that they actually sold intoxicating drinks. It seemed that they were ashamed to display this weakness: a relic of Puritan ancestry perhaps? Or is it an attitude left over from Prohibition, when drink had to be sold as a dark secret?

In hotels one finds a huge cavernous room, generally furnished with settees and armchairs in dark red velvet and what appear to be old masters on the walls. I even once saw a bookcase, though without a torch it would have been an impossibility to read. Often there were enormous pillars which appeared to serve no useful purpose, except perhaps to discourage the waiter from serving me because I was out of sight.

Canadians do not seem to like standing at the bar to drink, and one never sees them clustered around six deep as drinkers are in a popular English pub. There they look as though at last they have found their spiritual home, considerably more expensive, though, than their eventual one. I was told by one of the waiters that not so long ago it was illegal to stand at the bar; but I get the impression that even *sitting* down to drink is something that should not be exposed to the light of day.

I did a tour of Vancouver's celebrated Stanley Park. The weather was as cold and windy as in my home town of Hove, and that's usually very windy indeed, much to Albert's disgust; he can't stand being buffeted. I rather like it; it makes me feel alive. The guide apologized for the park's untidiness. All the corporation men had been on strike for several weeks: refuse-collectors, road-sweepers and gardeners. But it was as nothing to the rubbish I have seen back in England even when they're not on strike.

The azaleas were glowing with colour, not only in the park but also in people's gardens. The soil must be right for their cultivation.

Driving through this lovely park, full of old paths and tracks, colossal leafy trees and plants of every kind, magnificent views of the harbour and mountains, I could not help feeling what a paradise it must have been for the Indians who once were the only people to live there; how bitterly they must have resented being driven out to the barren lands. But I kept such thoughts to myself. The only evidence of them now is the Totem Park. Here are assembled a collection of totem poles, grotesquely but beautifully carved. One was almost a hundred feet tall. An Australian sitting behind me in the coach, ignoring our guide, proceeded to give all of us the benefit of his knowledge of totem poles, what they represented, and why. I wouldn't have minded five minutes of his dissertation, but after fifteen minutes I became somewhat irritated, especially as his knowledge of totem poles was confined to those he had seen in some museum or other. Never given to hiding my light under a bushel or averse from adding my quota to any topic, I interrupted the Australian, just as he was comparing these poles to the African ones he had seen. 'But it's not the same thing; these are Indians. Africans used theirs for quite different reasons. These totem poles were carved and erected to show what group the Indians belonged to.' Mind you, I was by no means sure of this, but I guessed that he wouldn't know either, in spite of his package tours. However, he and his wife were annoyed at my having the temerity to contradict this amateur Marco Polo, so they vehemently denied that totem poles were different here.

I think that the other passengers were more interested in the argument than in the subject of it. As for our guide, he just adopted the I-have-heard-it-all-before attitude; which indeed he probably had. Besides, I expect that he thought he wasn't paid to intervene in a passenger dispute; he might have got assaulted by this—by now irate—Australian.

Stanley Park is described in the guide-book as 'one of the finest city parks in the world, if not the finest, comparing not unfav-ourably with the Bois de Boulogne in Paris'. I wonder what we say about our parks. I must get a book and find out. Admittedly the Canadian parks are lovely, perhaps because they are not so short of land as we are.

The Indians who had once lived there were a very artistic group, called the Haida. When I asked the guide if there were any left now, he said that if there were they would be on the reservation. Up spoke the man from Australia again, to inform us that all of this land had belonged to the Indians; that they had been killed or driven out by land-seeking immigrants. This time I did not get involved in his argument. It seemed to me that the time to discuss the disappearance and extermination of the American Indian was not when one was a guest in the country. In any case, the Australians' record with the aborigines is not exactly a model of how to treat the indigenous population: even though a great many other countries, including our own, have some pretty dark spots to hide in that respect.

We went over the Lions' Gate Suspension Bridge. This is rather similar to the Golden Gate Bridge in San Francisco, but narrower. 'Too narrow for the traffic,' said our guide, 'but that's because there was only five million dollars available to build it. Most of that came from the Guinness Company. Not that they cared a hoot whether we wanted a bridge. No, it was for them, so that they could develop properties on the other side.'

'Why is it called Lions' Gate Bridge?'

'Oh, just because of those two carved lions at each end. I think that they were rejects from some exhibition. So rather than throw them away, they got stuck on the bridge. *We* call it the "Bridge that Beer built", that goes well with Vancouver's other name, the

"Burg that Booze built".' At this there was a chorus of questions from the passengers as to why it was called by that name. The driver said, 'Go on, you don't want to hear that old story,' knowing full well we did, and knowing also that he intended to tell us. 'A rip-roaring ex-river-boat captain set up a shop with a barrel of whiskey and scored an immediate success—even allowing for what he drank of it. Eventually he opened another shop, then a hotel, named the location Gastown, then changed it to Granville. At the request of the Canadian Pacific Railway this got changed to Vancouver Island; they thought nobody would want to travel to a place with an unknown name like Granville.'

I must say, all this was a lot more fun to hear than dreary statistics about the size of the population, height of their tallest building, or how many insurance companies they have.

We went to British Columbia University but there were no students as it was vacation time. The university is set among some of the loveliest scenery. The buildings themselves were just functional, with no pretence to style, but this was hardly noticeable, sited as they were amid splendid leafy trees, shrubs and beautifully-kept gardens. As for the homes of the residents, I have never seen such spaciousness, such a prodigal display of wealth or such huge gardens, where obviously there is no land shortage.

Michael asked me, in a nonchalant way, if I would like to see a real live rodeo? Somewhat incautiously I said I would, never thinking that there actually was one available.

'Good, I thought it would be another treat for you. There's a rodeo at a place called Cloverdale, about ten miles from here. We'll go this afternoon.'

Immediately Michael said this I could tell that he had already decided to see the rodeo. Why, I don't know, as it's very definite that he has no affinity with bucking broncos. Nevertheless, I was curious to see what actually did happen, having seen so many rodeos on the films. There, it looks a highly dangerous occupation, and sure needs to be lucrative—it may well be a very short career.

The roads were full of every kind of vehicle on the way there— cars, vans and jeeps, the drivers all yelling greetings to each other.

And the crowd when we got there! One great mass, just like Derby Day, and about as noisy.

My attention was focused on the handsome virile men, sun-tanned, broad-shouldered, and all wearing those ten-gallon hats. Heavens, what a dream come true! I would have loved to take one home. Naturally enough, Michael wasn't so enamoured; he very soon dragged me off to watch the events. Those bucking broncos were like live wire; it was astounding that the cowboys could even get *on* them, let alone stay on for several seconds—as they had to do to get points. Even more hazardous did it seem when they had to rope a calf, jump off the horse, throw the calf to the ground and tie it up. What heroes they were! Still, I suppose they wouldn't make such good husbands. Marriage isn't en-hanced by a knowledge of bronco-riding and calf-busting—at least I can't see where these pursuits fit in a home. As for riding the Brahma bulls, all the money in the world would never have tempted me. These bulls are supposed to be more mean-tempered than ordinary bulls. Whether this is true or not I don't know. Personally, as I am too nervous to walk through a field of cows, you can be sure that my knowledge of a bull's disposition is neg-ligible. The cowboys had to stay on the animals for eight seconds, without touching the bull with their free hand. This is certainly a country where men are men. If only I had been here years ago!

Most of all I enjoyed the chuck-wagon races. I'm sure that the chariot race in Ben-Hur wasn't more exciting. I didn't know anybody in the race, but I got just as keen as though I were personally involved.

Afterwards Michael insisted on our wandering around—he really likes this sort of thing—probably it gives him a feeling of solidarity with the masses. *I* always have liked crowds, wherever I am. Everything was designed to part you from your money in the shortest possible time. Pop-corn, ices, balloons and every other trifle had their sellers; there were rifle-ranges, bingo and, needless to say, the machines to risk your life on. Some of these made me dizzy just to look at them, so dangerous did they seem. Just fancy, paying out real money to be frightened out of your life! I had already made up my mind that nothing would induce me to venture on even the mildest of these—so why did I? Sometimes I believe that Michael mesmerizes me. Although he knew that I suffered from vertigo, he tried his utmost to make me have a ride on the huge wheel. Indeed, a great part of his time was devoted to trying to get me to the top of high buildings, perhaps on the assumption that a continuous diet of fear would eventually effect a cure—but that's a fallacy. I was at last persuaded to ride on a contraption that, although it never left the ground, whirled round and round like a dervish. Such gyrations were made even faster by Michael's exertions. I was too terrified to speak. When I staggered off after what seemed like an eternity, all Michael said was, 'It will give you something to write about.' It's so nice to be out with such a charming young man. A few more such experiences and I would be too shattered ever to write again. As it was, going back in the taxi I was speechless.

Every car here had on its number-plate the words, 'Beautiful British Columbia'. Even from the little that I saw, it is indeed a beautiful place.

I got into conversation with some vociferous American ladies in our hotel who had just finished a lightning Baedeker tour of Europe, and so considered themselves well-travelled. One of them, much bejewelled and made-up, practically overwhelmed me physically by putting her arms around me—which did not in the least endear her to me—and verbally by the torrent of useless information as to what I should see and do. 'You must take a coach trip to see Chaucer Lane and Anne Hathaway's Cottage; it's a replica of the one at Stratford-on-Avon. The whole scene is a bit of old England.'

Now why on earth should she imagine that I would want to travel all these miles just to see a bit of what I had left behind? She knew that I was English. So I replied, and it was a great effort to be polite, 'I have seen Anne Hathaway's Cottage—at Stratford-on-Avon—and Shakespeare's house too. Also I have read most of his plays; have you read them?'

'Good heavens, no. Couldn't read all that dreary old-fashioned language; he's too dated, and it takes too long to get the sense of it. Life's too short for all that high-falutin' talk.'

I could imagine these ladies, as colourful as parrots and with voices as shrill, scuttling around that old, and in my opinion, unspoiled town, Shakespeare's birthplace, gesticulating and uttering cries of, 'How quaint! How medieval! What a picture of

Old England!' and yet they had never bothered to read so much as one of the immortal plays. Ah well, I suppose they were harmless enough.

I shall always remember the last evening in Vancouver. It started off quietly enough with Michael and me having our usual drink in the bar. But in some strange way we collected around us such an assortment of nationalities—Irish, German, Swedish, Americans and Indians—India Indians, not Red—that very soon our table was like a miniature League of Nations. People over there really did like my accent, so that encouraged me in talk—not that I need much urging in that direction, or so I'm told.

The Irishman—'call me Pat'—came from Quebec and was very downright and anti-British, especially about our monarchy. 'It's an archaic and out-dated form that does no good to the country at all, but is kept in luxury at the tax-payers' expense.' (Why should he worry? He paid nothing.) 'Its sole purpose in life is to provide figureheads appearing from time to time to open this or that, a proceeding that could be done by anybody. They have no real power so why continue to have a monarchy? The history of your royalty, where Canada is concerned, is one of aggression.'

Unfortunately for me, this Pat knew a lot more about the history of Quebec (all to the detriment of the English) from the capture of Quebec by Wolfe in 1759, the abolition of French law and the suppression of the Catholics, to the capture in 1760 of Montreal—also by the bloody British. As for what the British had done to his home country, Ireland, that wonderful green island, that home of poets, and dreamers—the British had murdered it.

'When were you last in Ireland?' I somewhat sarcastically enquired.

'Sure, I haven't been there since I was a kid, but it's still the loveliest isle in creation.'

What balderdash he talked. I have noticed with a lot of these expatriates that they speak in lyrical terms of their own country but nothing would induce them even to visit it, let alone live there. Nevertheless, I thought better of arguing with an Irishman.

Michael was talking to the German in his own language, which irritated me, as I hadn't a clue what they were discussing. Nils from Sweden was fairly young and blond and radiated that particularly Swedish appearance of good health and cleanliness. He said that he came from Gotland and seeing my uncomprehending look told me it was an island in the Baltic. 'Surely you've heard of it?' My geographical knowledge of Sweden and the Baltic being practically nil, I couldn't pretend that I did know of his birthplace. Otherwise, if I could have got away with it, I'd have made out it was my second home, just to ingratiate myself with such a handsome man. Nils knew of Brighton; it's surprising how many people from thousands of miles distant seem to know Brighton.

Elmer, from Idaho, was interested to know what we thought about America, back in England. I was continually being asked this question. How could I explain that, to my knowledge, apart from politicians and people who have business interests there, ninety-five per cent of us never think about America at any time? We are far too concerned with the struggle to live in our own country. Sometimes I did get the impression that by neglecting to think constantly of America, we exposed ourselves to all sorts of dangers and misrepresentations.

Elmer went into a lengthy discourse and explained to me how generous Americans were; how freely they poured out money and goods for under-developed countries; how many Americans lived in these countries purely to teach the natives how to manufacture and modernize. I pointed out that was precisely what we had done years ago and now we were execrated as money- and land-grabbers, colonialists and imperialists; and that Americans had called us these names too. Now it was their turn to be misunderstood. They might imagine that because they were fighting against what they considered Communism the free world would love them, but a lot of people see America as an aggressor, and as for President Nixon, words fail them. Poor Elmer, he was somewhat overwhelmed by me, for all he could answer was, 'Have another drink.'

Goodness knows just what I was drinking, as everybody seemed to order their own special brand, so the drinks were weird and varied. I do recollect that they were ordering drinks with names like Harvey Warbanger and Ferdy Fluck-Pucker. By the look on the barman's face when asked to mix the former, I believe it was practically lethal.

Halfway through the evening Michael gave up all hopes of seeing that I didn't mix my drinks. He really hadn't a hope in heaven, with all those lovely men so eager to talk and provide me with a constant succession of free concoctions. To myself I said, somewhat bemused I'll admit, 'This is it. You are really appreciated at last.'

We sat around the table solving all the world's problems in a wonderful golden glow of peace and goodwill to all. Even Pat forgot to be belligerent, and although he still kept calling us the 'bloody British' there was no malice behind it. Later on, at 2 a.m., I discovered the party had increased by the addition of two females. How they got there was a mystery; most assuredly I didn't invite them—not likely! I was having far too good a time being the one and only female. These occasions are few and far between.

By 3 a.m., Michael had disappeared, simply abandoned me and thrown me to the wolves, metaphorically speaking. Luckily they weren't the man- or woman-eating variety. Michael and his German friend had no doubt retired to discuss in private such soul-stirring matters as the rise and fall of the Third Reich. At least I charitably assumed that this was the urgent reason for their not even staying to see that I reached my room in safety.

My Swedish friend, Nils, escorted me to my door with great panache and kissed my hand before departing, with many assurances that we would meet again. Of course we never did. Such an occasion cannot be repeated. Neither would I want it to be.

For about the first time in my life I got up with a bad head, no doubt occasioned by an injudicious mixture of cocktails of the world and only four hours' sleep. It took a great effort even to lift my head from the pillow. 'Never again, not if I know it,' was my first thought. 'I must have been mad.' But if I was groggy, you should have seen Michael. At first I didn't even recognize him. An apparition appeared in the lobby, a pallid wraith, greenish-hued of face, barely able to stand upright, totally uncomprehending where he was. Indisposed as I was, I could have died with laughter at the sight of him—if only I had dared.

I shudder to think what my nephew thought of us; he had

come over especially to drive us to the airport. I sat in the front with Nick as I knew that Michael was incapable of uttering a sensible, or pleasant, word. Just to pile on the agony I turned round at intervals to let Michael know how much farther we had to go. He didn't thank me for the information.

Nick was an angel. He carried our heavy cases right into the airport. Michael, at his dying gasp, just managed to make it to the nearest bar, to have a hair of the dog that bit him.

How very fortunate that we were travelling on the 'Champagne Flight', where champagne is given free—several glasses if you want it, and we did, for other reasons than the prestige attached to drinking champagne on an aeroplane. It took more than one glass before Michael became human again.

10: Minneapolis

For some obscure reason I did not much care for Minneapolis. Perhaps I was still feeling the effects of the hangover; or perhaps it was because the hotel, the Sheraton Ritz, was convinced that they had never received a reservation for our rooms, and seemed less than eager for our company. Every hotel was full because the Metropolitan Opera was performing in the city, and all the high and mighty had come from far and wide to show that they could appreciate this musical feast. Michael was an absolute hero and a tower of strength, flatly refusing to go into the wilderness and search for a hotel with rooms to spare. I would have been no good at all against the opposition. Mind you, when it was eventually sorted out, I was left with a small room high up, and no shower in the bathroom, while Michael was on the third floor up, with a larger room and all amenities. But then he doesn't function properly unless all is for his comfort, so it was as well that he should have the best.

I think that all this haggling gave me an aversion to the city before I had even seen it. Not that losing reservations is confined to America; it's done in England too. Shortly before I left England I was lunching with an American who bitterly complained about the perfidy of our hotels. Not only had the hotel, where he had made a reservation nearly three months ago, informed him that they had no knowledge of such a booking, but also the one that finally he managed to book had no shower in the bathroom, no air-conditioning and, worst crime of all, they didn't serve a glass of ice-water with his breakfast. Why do Americans have this mania for drinking ice-cold water? Every time that I wanted something to eat, even if it was only a hamburger, immediately a glass of this stuff was put in front of me as though I had just traversed the Sahara and must be dying of thirst.

This is another state which proclaims its beauty or other advantage on the number plates of cars; I had already seen, 'Beautiful British Columbia', and 'Arizona Grand Canyon State'; now it was 'Minnesota, State of 10,000 Lakes'. Why don't we have something similar on our cars? We could have 'Surrey, the Commuters' Paradise', 'Sussex by the Sea', 'Kent for Hops and Beer'. I'm sure it would make driving on motorways less dreary.

What an astonishing thing it was to find that the Mississippi River, that I had last seen in New Orleans over two thousand miles away, was again to be seen here in Minneapolis!

In my schooldays, I remember what a bore it was having to learn about rivers and being told that the Mississippi was the longest river in the world. The immensity of it never meant anything at that time. This time I was determined to sail on the river aboard the sternwheel vessel named *Jonathan Padeford*. It was designed to look like a nineteenth-century paddle-wheeler, and Michael discovered that the boat started from the twin city of St Paul. But when we arrived at the pier it was to discover that the owner of the boat had decided not to run any more trips that day, in spite of the fact that it was advertised in the newspaper that he sailed three times every day. How very nice and convenient to be able to pack up work just whenever you feel like it, regardless of the fact that some people have come a considerable distance just to sail on your boat! In the taxi back to the hotel I asked the driver if he could pack it in whenever the mood took him. 'If I did that I'd never do any work at all. I'm in the mood for non-work practically every day.'

It really was a disappointment to miss floating along on the Mississippi for the second time. I had visualized myself singing, a long way after Paul Robeson, 'Old Man River' and such-like melodies from *Showboat*. Though probably if I had done so, the captain, hearing this unfamiliar noise, would have turned back, thinking something was wrong with the engines. As for Michael, he characteristically told me, 'I wouldn't have dreamt of coming with you if I had had any idea that you might try to sing.' Talk about deflation!

Although Minneapolis and St Paul are known as the Twin Cities, because they are so close together, St Paul, the capital of Minnesota, seemed to have a different character from Minneapolis, rather old-fashioned and stately.

I had always visualized the American Mid West as a rather barren plain inhabited by a primitive cultureless people. It was nothing like that here; in fact, the Twin Cities appeared to be very pleasant places in which to live. Not that the weather was pleasant. It rained steadily all the next morning, and as Minneapolis seems to be full of trees that droop dismally when their branches get water-logged, it was impossible to walk far without resembling a drowned cat. As I was soon bored with staying in my room, just gazing at the rain and complaining about it to Michael, he hired a luxurious Chevrolet, just for me, so that I could view some of the ten thousand lakes in comfort.

I saw four lakes, so huge that they were more like inland seas than lakes. They were beautiful, with lush grass around and huge trees with their branches dipping into the water. But to some extent, when you have seen one lake you have seen them all, so I told the driver not to bother with the other 9,996, which greatly relieved him. He told me he was sick to death of showing people the lakes, and was also fed up with Minneapolis in general; the people were culturally about as wet as the rain dripping from the trees. Finding that I really listened to his diatribe— probably very few of his passengers did take notice—he went on, 'I was born here, but give me Chicago any time. You risk getting shot up there, but the city is alive. Here the people are too lethargic to lift a gun even if they had one.' Personally he much preferred Australia to America and so did his wife. Naturally, always after information, I asked why. 'I worked there for five years. It's a more advanced country. Why, they had votes for women in 1902'—not that he believed in all this freedom for women and only over his dead body would his wife go out to work, he added. As for everybody thinking that America had the highest standard of living in the world it was all bosh; he was far better off in Australia. At least it wasn't a country peopled by all the throw-outs and rejects who, unable to make a go of it in their own country, came over here to live on Relief.

'No,' I nearly said, 'Australia was peopled by convicts, who were transported there because England threw them out.' But I thought it politic to keep quiet, just as I also refrained from asking him why, if Australia was such a paradise, he hadn't stayed there. I reckoned that he was about the most un-American American that I had met so far. Still, he certainly knew his way around the city. We covered miles of country, with wide avenues of trees and green fields. In fact Minneapolis appeared, as far as the scenery was concerned, the greenest city that I had seen. I remarked on this to the driver, who muttered, 'So it should be; it rains nearly every day.'

The different types of house were very pleasant to look at. Here again, as I had seen before in America, was street after street of houses all different from each other. And yet although the symmetry was lost, the effect was very pleasing. It seemed as though each owner had waited to see the style of his neighbour's house, and then had his built quite dissimilar. I cannot really describe the architecture. There was one house like a miniature crenellated castle, another tiered and coloured like a pink wedding-cake. There were Tudor, Gothic, Spanish and Dutch houses in an absolute medley. And yet in some incomprehensible way they all harmonized. I couldn't help feeling that some of this variety back in England might be a good idea. It would be a pleasant change from housing-estates where everything is built exactly alike. Unless you know your way around these estates in the dark, you can get lost as easily as you can in the Hampton Court Maze.

I tentatively suggested to Michael that we should visit the Minnehaha Falls, but he showed no great enthusiasm at the prospect; probably he knows nothing about Hiawatha. Not that I recollect the reams of that poem I had to learn in school with any great pleasure, but it would have been interesting to view the source of Longfellow's inspiration and my suffering.

What a lot of conventions they seem to have in America! Almost every hotel has its quota of back-slapping, full-of-bonhomie men, all wearing enormous soup-plate badges that proclaim their identity. They assemble in the lobby of the hotel in the morning and then disappear all day. The wives, left alone, also congregate.

Most of them look bored to tears—probably suffering from a surfeit of conferences. They also wear badges of hideous design. Nothing would induce me to venture out similarly labelled, advertising to all and sundry that I belonged to my husband and his organization. In the evening, the men emerge, even more jolly than before and endeavour to console the forlorn wives, their own included.

Michael got really irritated at this exhibition of American gettogetherness. He refused to dine in the hotel—it's not all honey to be with him, as he is far from being the personification of sweetness at times. He found a German restaurant, the Heidelburg; a most attractive place with beamed ceiling, leaded-light windows and a huge open-hearted fireplace. It was run, or owned, by a very warm and friendly lady who was interested in hearing about England in general and me in particular.

Michael ordered German beer; it came in huge glasses and was very good indeed. Because Michael appears to be *en rapport* with Germans and their food I let him choose for me. He recommended for the main course a delicious dish; I believe it was called *sauerbraten hassenpfeffer*; I consumed so much of it that I couldn't manage the apfel-strudel, unfortunately. Good food, pleasant surroundings, very quiet music all added up to a most enjoyable evening, I must admit.

We were leaving for Chicago the next day, and, having breakfast in the morning—on my own as usual, since I have long ago discarded any thoughts of Michael being a companionable breakfaster—I looked around at the other people, mostly men at this early hour. I was interested to note the lack of class distinctions. Obviously wealthy businessmen were on Christian name terms with the waiters, without any air of doing them a personal favour by being so friendly. At one table near to me the waiter was sitting down for a few moments and talking about politics to the guest as though there were no difference between a wealthy businessman and a hotel waiter. I did in fact find this lack of class distinction almost everywhere I went, and to me it was one of the attractive aspects of American life. I just couldn't imagine the same thing happening in England. Perhaps it is because America hasn't an aristocracy as we know it. The wealthy and upper-class never emigrated; they had no need to; they were doing all right in their own country. No, it was the poor and ignorant, the refugees who came to this haven, and it is their children and grandchildren who have made America. Not that I haven't seen and heard as arrogant expressions of superiority from some Americans as ever I have heard from some of the British aristocracy. The acquisition of power, whether gained or inherited, seems to bring out the worst in some people.

11: Chicago

I discovered that Chicago was different from what I had imagined it to be. I visualized a kind of concrete jungle where one had to face the hazard of ricocheting bullets and be terrified by the noise of screaming police sirens. My imagination went back to all those gangster films I had seen of Dillinger and Capone, for ever exterminating their enemies with sawn-off shot-guns. Chicago wasn't a bit like that, though I did think that the police looked very formidable with their holstered pistols on one side and deadly-looking truncheons on the other. When they stood in the middle of the road directing the traffic I can assure you that I made no attempt to cross against the lights.

Our hotel was on La Salle Street, the financial centre of Chicago, and so always full of people. It had the usual vast and opulent lobby; the Americans seem to have the idea of putting all their goods in the shop window, so to speak. Because it was one of the older hotels with good solid walls it was very quiet upstairs. I prefer this type to the shiny glass and chromium new ones where one is continually waking to the sound of the lavatory flushing in the next room, or unable to sleep because a near-by television is blaring forth.

I visited the Art Institute of Chicago which I had been told was so famous that directors of other museums came there just to stand, and stare, and envy. I must admit that I didn't see anything very marvellous about it; the paintings were much the same as those I had looked at elsewhere, though there were some old masters that I didn't know existed, and wonderful French paintings. Unfortunately, I am not greatly enamoured of spending hours gazing at paintings; after a few hours my feet remind me that they have had enough of walking. Besides, there are only a few artists that I really go mad about.

Certainly the artist Miro—I suppose one does call him an artist —is not appreciated by me. All his drawings remind me of the Exhibition of Children's Paintings that is sponsored by the *Daily Mirror*, except that with children there is the impression of a free art form, naïve and charming. I am not so devoid of a knowledge of art that I decry all experimental forms as crude and unsound, but Miro's art-form seems to me to be not just lunatic fringe, but lunacy itself. And when one reads in the catalogue that 'his shapes keep their integrity as individualized forms despite their metamorphic transformations', what on earth does all that mean in plain language? All I could see were crude figures, drawn as young children do them, with lines for arms and legs. An American family was also gazing at this 'art', when one of the children said, 'Mam, that's just like I drew in school yesterday.'

I cannot but feel that, for the older generation at any rate, such art-forms make us feel that the perpetrator had his tongue in his cheek when he exhibited such stuff. In my wildest dreams I could never see these paintings some hundred years hence being auctioned at Christie's or Sotheby's, or the public being asked to subscribe to keep them from leaving England. I would certainly subscribe to have them taken abroad.

Even the solid forms were incomprehensible. I fail to understand how a red stool with an empty green box standing on it could in the remotest way be called 'Monsieur and Madame'. Or how another stool with a wooden egg on it could be another 'Monsieur and Madame'. Or how an indeterminate lump of what appeared to be concrete with an ordinary wooden spoon sticking out of the top could be 'A Woman'. These farcical objects had been lent by some other gallery. If they had been mine I'd have parted with them permanently.

I really thought that the public would be convinced that this tripe had no value whatever, that a dollar would buy you something better, so I was somewhat taken aback to hear a very formidable lady, and very knowledgeable too by the sound of her, explaining to her husband that these ludicrous and grotesque forms were allegorical and meant to induce one's own emotional experience. From the bored look on his face his emotional experience was non-existent, but as he repeated, 'Yes, dear, I see, dear,' at frequent intervals, she appeared to be satisfied. When she asked me my opinion, I'm afraid that, confronted with such firmness of character and forceful opinions, my moral courage deserted me. Far from proclaiming that at best I thought Miro was joking, and at the worst the pictures were hideous, I said, 'Well, it makes you think doesn't it?' After all, I wasn't telling a lie.

This city seemed more American to me than any other I have seen so far. Also it seemed a man's city. I don't exactly know why, unless it is all the business buildings, or the air that people have of getting somewhere fast.

I went on a Gray Line Tour of Chicago; it was fascinating. I saw the 'Wigwam' where Abraham Lincoln was nominated for the Presidency; the Biograph Theatre where John Dillinger was shot; the hotel that Al Capone owned and lived in; I felt that I too was living dangerously. I also looked at what the driver assured us was the original church of Moody, of Moody and Sankey fame. Whether it was or not, I don't know; I had found, through repeated questions as to the name of particular buildings, that most of the people who lived in the city had no idea what they were. Of course, it's the same in England. Ask a Londoner how to get to a certain place; he hasn't a clue; he knows only the part where he lives.

All this talk of churches made my seat-companion, a very talkative American lady, launch forth into anecdotes of her churchgoing days. 'Every Sunday all nine of us marched in a crocodile in front of Ma and Pa, and not one of us dared look round or talk out loud; in fact we weren't allowed to speak for the entire morning.' Perhaps she was making up for it now.

In our Sunday School, the teacher was always telling us never to worry our parents to buy us this or that because we would find that the 'Lord will provide'. I used to wish that He would demonstrate by even a small token how much and what He meant to provide. I suppose the teacher meant that He would provide in heaven, but I didn't want to die of starvation before I got there.

We drove along Lakeshore Drive. On one side was Lake Michigan and on the other were apartment houses where millionaires live; our driver said that it's known as 'The Gold Coast', or 'Lake Shore Drive Condominium'; I didn't like to ask what that word meant.

There is a most ingenious device for regulating the flow of traffic. Instead of dividing the six lanes so that there are three going and coming, there is a kerb between each lane that can be raised or lowered hydraulically. In the morning it's worked so that there are four lanes going into Chicago and two out; in the evening it's altered so that four lanes leave the city and only two head in.

The lake was full of lovely yachts, and, although such a short distance from the city, the shore was so full of people sitting in the sun that it resembled an English seaside town. I would never have thought that a city could have such a beautiful water-front.

As Chicago came into view again it was a dramatic sight; the towering cliffs of sky-scrapers, although man-made, were awe-inspiring.

In the evening, as usual, when the question arose as to where we should have dinner, Michael had not the least idea where to go. Chicago is not noted for good restaurants, so I solved Michael's problem by suggesting a French one. As there were only about five of these we picked on Jacques. It had a patio garden with sliding roof, but we sat in the dining-room. The food was very good indeed and the atmosphere very romantic. Soft lights and sweet music—played by a string trio—induced a feeling in me of peace and goodwill to all men. (I wonder why men only?) All it seemed to induce in Michael was a soporific feeling; at least it did until he saw the bill, at the sight of which he appeared to be stunned. Well, there you are. One may sing that 'the best things in life are free' but I have never found it so. In America, as in England, they have to be paid for.

I simply had to have my hair done and I was agreeably surprised at the friendliness and low cost of a shampoo and set. While waiting in the hairdresser's, I got into conversation with three ladies, all, I reckon, in their late fifties. When they realized that I was English I was overwhelmed by all their conversation about how they had loved visiting England last year. They had been in several of our famous country houses and even shaken hands with a lord. I was a bit sceptical of this in view of the fact that they couldn't remember his name. I'm sure that I would never forget shaking hands with a real live lord.

All three of these ladies were widows; I really was amazed at the multitude of middle-aged widows that I met in America. Whatever happens to the husbands to cause them to die off so early in life? As these ladies were very lively and friendly, I asked them about this.

'Oh, we kill them off young here. American husbands work very hard to provide their wives with every conceivable luxury—so that when they are gone, the wives won't suffer.'

'Don't you suffer then from being a widow? In England widows are at a disadvantage inasmuch as they don't get asked out as they did when they had a husband.'

'You don't suffer here if you are a widow with money. There is so much one can do—join clubs, go on a cruise, see the rest of America, which is what we three are now doing.'

'Yes, but don't you miss the company of your husbands?'

'What company?' they said. 'We hardly ever saw them. Business kept them for hours in the office and even at home they were on the telephone all the time; conversation was a dead duck.'

When I tentatively suggested that perhaps they could have persuaded their husbands not to work such long hours, they hooted with derision and strongly denied being able to influence them at all.

'We know that you all in England think that we have a matriarchal society and that our men are hen-pecked. But it isn't so. They do just what they like where business is concerned.'

'And precious little of what we like after business,' added Sally. 'They were always too tired.' The laughter that followed left no doubt as to what their husbands had failed to do.

'You simply don't understand Americans,' Lucy told me. (By this time we were on first-name terms.) 'They can't slow down, because big business is their life. They would pass away even earlier if they had to slow down or retire. Their work is their pleasure. That, and seeing us well-dressed and groomed.'

Dolly added her quota. 'It's not like your country where there is a leisured class with dozens of servants to wait on them, hand and foot.'

I endeavoured to explain that their conception of the English aristocracy was a bit out-dated; that very few people nowadays kept retinues of servants; those were lucky who could employ a 'daily', but I don't think that they believed me, or perhaps they didn't want to be disillusioned in their idea of the 'old country'.

I found that a lot of Americans take credit for being different from those born with a 'silver spoon in their mouth'. Perhaps wealthy Americans, who really have made it by their own efforts, and not through inheritance, do take a pride and pleasure in their unremitting task of acquiring the visible evidence of prosperity.

These ladies never referred to the 'death' or 'dying' of their husbands. It was always, 'he passed on' or 'passed away'. Is it that the word death is so final, whereas 'passed on' seems to imply that the departed has only temporarily left his wealth and social status? I frequently saw, outside what appeared to be ordinary houses, a notice saying 'Funeral Home'. I should have thought that the last thing the departed needed was another earthly home—having so recently left his own. As for the cemeteries! Well, the weight and size of the gravestones are such as to make one believe that once you are down, you stay down. And such huge and elaborate sculptures—angels with out-stretched wings, children with their arms raised to heaven; there were horrors of plaster and of marble, and I even found one that appeared to be made of plastic. Why do they erect these monu-ments, with all the departed one's virtues inscribed on the stone? Surely if you believe that your loved one is going to heaven, he doesn't need this obelisk to record his passing? And if you don't believe, well, it's a waste of time and money, anyway.

Or is death an American's only link with reality? To know that when you are gone from a world that perhaps hardly knew you were there, your tombstone records you for all eternity. Generations ahead will read your name, will know that you breathed, you lived, you died. One of the most macabre sights, or it appeared so to me, was an inscription on a gravestone, 'To the beloved memory of Helen aged 21, and to her father, born 1920, died   ? '. The father isn't dead yet but his name is inscribed on the stone and needs only the date. I just found it impossible to visualize putting flowers on a daughter's grave and reading your own name also.

In England there just is not enough room for everybody to have six feet of earth. And yet, I do remember that a visit to the cemetery was a Sunday-afternoon pleasure: there were so many well-kept graves, so many widows and mothers, just remembering. We all come into the world with so little ceremony that surely it does no harm to leave it with some dignity. If it does nothing else, to see a funeral procession go by must remind us of our mortality.

Later on I wandered around the streets admiring the buildings. These towered on either side—steel and glass, very plain and functional, yet somehow teeming with energy.

Chicagans seem mildly satirical about their city. I asked a man in the street the way to the John Hancock Center, and he said, 'Madam, you just don't want to put yourself out to see that place. One look and you will know that it was designed by a colour-blind and cross-eyed architect. It's too big, too black and too ugly.' Really he was too denigrating. Black it certainly is, but also majestic and a planner's dream. I liked this city, it seemed so full of life.

In front of the civic centre there is a Picasso metal sculpture, resembling nothing known to me. Determined to find out more about it, I asked an official what it represented. He was a very polite and helpful gentleman, prepared to spend time on a foreigner. 'You would like to know what it is?' he said. 'Well now, only God, and presumably Picasso—though that's open to doubt—know. Some people call it X, the unknown quantity; some say it reminds them of their mother-in-law; others say that it's just a few chunks of metal that Picasso wanted to get rid of.'

'What do you think of it?' I enquired. But he was very wary and tactful. 'I think that it's whatever you want it to be. A symbol to suit your prevailing mood.'

The Museum of Science and Industry is an absolutely marvellous building and a paradise for children because there is so much for them to do—buttons to push to start the exhibits working, telephones that explain the most complicated experiments. I could have spent hours and hours there; in fact, my enthusiasm made Michael decide to visit the place. I noticed that if *he* wanted to go anywhere it was always all right for us to go together. But if it was somewhere that would have bored him, then somehow it changed to, 'You'll be much better able to describe it if you go on your own.' Not that he was any company, for he simply disappeared as soon as we got there. But the museum was fascinating —so huge, so well set-out, so very instructive and entertaining. There was an electric theatre that amazed one at just what could be done with electricity; a full-sized Mid-West farm; a blacksmith's shop in operation; a time-machine, and hundreds of other marvellous things. If I lived in Chicago I'd be going there every week.

As for the huge working lay-out of the Santa Fé Railway, it was every father's dream, with two long trains continually passing each other. I love trains. Whenever I see one go by, I have to watch it until it is out of sight. These modern trains are not half so exciting as the old steam ones, which always seemed to possess a life of their own. For instance they have often provided material for thrillers. Whoever heard of exciting events on a bus? *Murder on the Orient Express* wouldn't sound half so intriguing entitled *Murder on the No. 11 Bus*. When I was young, every train journey was something of an adventure, partly owing to the lights failing to function as the train entered a tunnel. So you sat in Stygian darkness with several strangers. As there were no corridors you couldn't leave the carriage. I remember once travelling to London and the only other person in the carriage was a middle-aged man. Going through the longest tunnel, suddenly, out went the lights. Then I felt a hand on mine and a quiet voice said, 'Don't be nervous; we will soon see daylight.' At that time I wasn't in the least afraid of being shut up with a man; with such a dearth of the species even one in the dark was better than none at all, but nowadays, if a man took my hand in the dark I should be extremely apprehensive as to what else he had designs on.

My last call in Chicago was to the *Sun–Times* Building, where one could look through glass to see the presses working, a sight new to me. I expect that, if I asked, I could see the presses in London, but it wouldn't seem the same thing at all.

A most helpful man in the long corridor, also like me a visitor, explained at great length and detail how it was all done. I was so entranced by his honeyed voice that I never took in half he said. Afterwards, over a cup of coffee he told me that he lived just outside Chicago, and also how many murders had been committed in the last month. This caused me some alarm. I think that it was about sixteen and only two of the criminals had been caught.

He was one of the few Americans that I met who didn't get chauvinistic about his state, and about Chicago itself he was very satirical. The cabs were dirty and dear; the restaurants had no idea of good food; and as for the wind—that which blew over the Russian Steppes was as nothing to the wind that blew off Lake Michigan. Yet, he had to confess, he couldn't live anywhere else. I too felt the lure of Chicago; I felt at home in it far more than in New York.

My new-found friend invited me to his home to meet his wife and family. Given time enough I would have liked that; but time was getting on and even Michael might have felt some faint stirrings of alarm if I was absent for too many hours.

12: Toronto

From Chicago we went to Toronto, certainly a very different city. In fact, it seemed to me that all three cities we visited in Canada resembled none that we had seen in America.

The people were far more English.

In America I had to keep on reminding myself that Americans were not English, in spite of speaking the same language; but here in Canada again it somehow felt like being in England.

Toronto used to be known as the pure city, not only because there was no pollution but because it was pure in art and morals. Now, like every other city, they have their quota of hippies and nude shows. The advertisements for these dubious attractions were many and varied, each one proclaiming their wares as the best; though the human anatomy allowing for very little variation, I don't see where is the difference.

One poster advertised 'real nudes': what this meant I couldn't fathom, as obviously they weren't wax models. Wax models remind me of the stage tableaux in which—in the non-permissive era—the girls were not allowed to move or bat an eyelid. We were far more interested in seeing if they could remain perfectly still than in realizing that they were nude. In any case the settings always seemed to mask discreetly those parts of the body that encouraged lubricity. I was told, but it may not have been true, that there is a place in Toronto where even the chef is nude, except for his tall hat. Why does he wear that I wonder? If it were true I would never eat there; I would feel that the chef's mind wasn't on his cooking.

As usual, Michael, like his predecessor, showed more interest in these establishments than in the surrounding architecture. Anyway, I hastily rushed him past these 'palaces of art'. I do feel that it's part of my duty while out here to look after the moral welfare of my escorts. The fact that they show no appreciation of my efforts on their behalf is beside the point—altruists and other benefactors the world over have often been reviled. There are so many societies for rescuing fallen women; and who pushes them? But where is there a society for rescuing fallen men? I think that I should start one.

Perhaps all this display of nudity makes men better as lovers, but I don't believe that it does much for them as husbands—on the contrary in fact, if a friend of mine is to be believed. Her husband has an insatiable desire to watch nude shows in Soho; but she says that by the time he gets home from one he is so exhausted by the appearance of sex that he has no desire to be loving with her. As for really possessing one of those topless and bottomless, he'd be hopeless.

On our first evening in the hotel I came downstairs and found Michael in conference with the bell-hop. 'He has told me of a very good place to dine, called Ed's Warehouse,' said Michael, 'it's only a hundred yards from here.'

I never learn. I should have known instinctively that Michael had no idea of distances. We walked for ever, about a mile at least, and the cold wind blew like a tornado, to the detriment of my appearance and temper. Eventually we arrived at Ed's Warehouse. The outside of the place did nothing to lighten my spirits; it was drab and uninspiring to say the least. But, after we had climbed an exceedingly scruffy staircase, we entered a highly civilized Edwardian restaurant. One end was a huge room, with very little in the way of furnishing; there they serve huge steaks. We chose the other room and the roast beef. Ed had furnished this end with red velvet upholstery, Tiffany lamp-shades, covered screens and very dim lighting—not to disguise the quality of the food which was very good. We were tucked away in a cosy little alcove, and such was the atmosphere that I almost expected to see Edward VII drinking champagne with a seductive chorus girl. The only feeling that marred my enjoyment was the thought of the long trudge back.

My first morning in Toronto! How very pleasant to have my breakfast brought into my room by a smiling waiter. He told me that the temperature would be 75° to 80°, just right for visiting Niagara. All that cold water cascading must make one feel one ought to be cool even if one isn't.

Naturally enough, I longed to visit Niagara Falls. I was told that this place was extremely popular with honeymoon couples, which rather surprised me. I would have thought that a place so full of people would not commend itself to a newly-married couple. Though, on reflection, it is perhaps a good idea; a honeymoon is often a great strain and even a bad start-off. For, after two or three days of complete isolation, conversation does tend to dry up, and even on a honeymoon love-making can't be a full-time occupation. Once the first transports of love are over, inevitably one finds that the partner is no great shakes at keeping one enlivened with witty remarks and after-dinner conversation; so then one begins to worry whether marriage will turn out a boring affair. In the event, of course, it is all right, because once the honeymoon is over, living together becomes as much of a habit as eating and drinking. The husband finds out that, if his wife is not very good at managing the household accounts, the old saying, 'Two can live as cheaply as one', is only applicable if one of them starves.

We had introductions to some extremely pleasant people in the publishing world, who were driving us to Niagara, about eighty miles from Toronto. The journey was along Queen Elizabeth Way; this had been opened by Queen Elizabeth, and a small column at one end commemorates the event. The falls were far more wonderful than I had visualized from photographs I had seen; one such, an immense wall of rushing water, is known as the Horseshoe Falls, an awe-inspiring sight. All that mighty volume of water falling from that height, sending up clouds of spray, was so fascinating to watch that it had a mesmeric effect on me. I felt as though I must keep on looking at it.

Surprisingly, just before the water fell over the edge it was a distinctly green colour—rather attractive I thought. Then I was told that the falls used to be crystal clear; it's pollution that causes the green. Fancy, pollution at Niagara!

What seemed like miles below in the gorge was a boat, *Maid of the Mist*. All the passengers wear oil-skin coats and hats, and have a trip along the river to get a close look at the bottom of the falls. I thought that I too might do this trip until I noticed that the boat sailed so close to the falls, right into the spray, that it got caught in the eddying water and rocked alarmingly.

There is a legend that in the spray you may see the lovely Indian maiden, Lelawala, Maid of the Mist. She was the last Indian maiden supposedly sacrificed to the harvest spirit, by being pushed over Horseshoe Falls. But I knew that if I was in that rocking boat my state of health would effectively stop my peering into the spray.

However, in spite of my claustrophobia, I did find enough courage to go down to what seemed the bowels of the earth. Here are tunnels that go to the back of the falls. We had to dress in rubber boots and long black rubber coats with black hoods. It really was an eerie experience down there, with all those dark, wet subterranean tunnels, and anonymous figures passing by like troglodytes shunning the light of day. But it was well worth overcoming my fear of dark enclosed places. The close-up view of the falls was marvellous, and the roar was deafening.

At one of the access points, I put my head right under that rushing cascade of cold water. Just like all the other tourists, I felt it was really a thrill to do this, though nothing would induce me to have a cold shower at home. However, with my usual vanity, I do feel a sense of one-upmanship; it's not everybody who can boast of putting their head under Niagara Falls.

It's not only the falls themselves that are worth looking at. The authorities have made the whole place very attractive. Of course, it's touristy but why not? At least all the crowds are there to enjoy themselves and not to be violent and aggressive.

Prospect Park is a very pleasant expanse of green grass and shady trees. One can sit on the benches and be lulled into sleep by the distant sound of the water. There is a funicular railway that goes up an extremely steep incline—I'm sure that it is 1-in-1—to the top of the cliff where one can get another view of the falls. Having but recently overcome claustrophobia I was not at all anxious to do the same for my vertigo. However, I was assured by Michael that it looked far steeper than it really was—a fallacious statement, as I discovered too late as usual. But, as there was no other visible means of getting to the top, I went. My imagination played with the thought of the appalling accident that would result if the cable broke, and also with the fact that we would have to descend this precipice by the same method. Starting from the top would be even more terrifying. As usual, I received no praise or encouragement for actually travelling on this hazardous contraption. But by now I was inured to suffering in silence, in fact even pretending that there is nothing in life I enjoy more than taking these appalling risks with my valuable person. But no amount of persuasion could get me to go in the Skylon. This is a tower that seems tall enough to reach the sky; but the terrifying part was that one ascended to this height by means of two elevators on the outside of the building. From where we were these elevators looked like oversized beetles crawling up and down; I felt faint just to look at them. Even if one was high enough up there to see heaven, I couldn't have attempted it. Honestly, I'd sooner climb Everest.

Years ago I read that Blondin, the French tightrope-walker, had, in 1859, crossed Niagara Falls on a rope tightly stretched across. In fact he did this several times, even blindfolded and wheeling a barrow. Never having seen the falls I didn't then realize what an almost incredible feat this was.

Farther up from the falls there was a suspension bridge over the river and people were actually queueing up to cross over, even dallying in the middle to enjoy the view. I never cease to marvel at these intrepid souls, but never think of joining them. The very word 'suspension' makes me suspicious of the safety of such a bridge. I prefer something more solid, built up from the ground.

However, as it was a beautiful spot, we stayed a while to consume the most excellent food that our hosts provided. It really was idyllic, far from the noise of the crowds, with the roar of the falls faintly in the distance.

To see Americans or Canadians picnicking is to be amazed at the size of the operation; one would think that they had prepared for a siege or an accident that would prevent them from returning to civilization for weeks. They seem to bring everything but the kitchen sink—folding chairs and tables, portable stoves, cutlery enough for a full-course meal, table-cloths, ice-boxes, sauces

—everything you could possibly require, and a lot that you couldn't—or so I thought. When I was on a coach trip in Los Angeles I even saw a family that had set up a barbecue, and the smoke and smell were polluting the countryside.

I did an early-morning television appearance with Ed Murray, a very nice and lively interviewer. He must have to get up at the crack of dawn to do his show, for I had to be there at 7.15 a.m. Because it was a television appointment, Michael decided he should be there too—if only to bask in my reflected glory. I would have preferred his absence; at 6.30 a.m., he is not an ideal companion.

I was also on a radio programme, and there was a cocktail party especially for me. I really felt honoured that not only was so much trouble taken to welcome a fleeting visitor but also that so many people there had read my books. Each time I encountered the hospitality and friendliness of people in America and Canada, I realized how reserved and insular we must appear to them.

The name Toronto is an Indian word meaning The Place of Meeting. In the seventeenth century the land was bought from the Indians for 149 barrels of goods. It seems an awful piece of chicanery, but it was at least a degree better than obtaining the land by exterminating the original inhabitants.

I have seen so much of America and Canada that is still practically empty of civilization. It is so green, so luxuriant and fertile, that all the time my imagination can visualize what a home it must have been for the Indians. No wonder they so bitterly resented the white race and fought with all the means at their disposal to keep their land.

Michael and I went to see a relic of Toronto's more immediate past. This was a castle called Casa Loma, built for Sir Henry Mill Pellat. He was born in 1859 and began his business career at fifteen years of age, eventually becoming a multi-millionaire. It seemed to me, from reading about him, that he had delusions of grandeur, visualizing himself as a knight of old rescuing beleaguered maidens from their baronial homes; for this huge ninety-eight-room castle, which to me appeared like some Gothic apparition out of Translyvania for a Bram Stoker background, full of vast towers and battlements, dungeons of basements and probably secret passages, was something never before seen in

Toronto—or anywhere else for that matter. One could have roasted a whole ox on the kitchen range; there were eleven baths and a shooting gallery, not to mention a marble swimming pool. The stables cost 250,000 dollars and every horse had had its name inscribed in gold on its stall. Eventually, Sir Henry could not afford to keep it up, and it became Toronto's white elephant. Now the Kiwanis Club have developed it as a tourist attraction. I suppose in England it would be labelled a 'folly'. But is it, and was Sir Henry foolish? It gave employment to hundreds; and much pleasure to the people who stayed there, and now it does the same for the thousands who go to see it.

There are lovely parks in Toronto, and I was amazed to read a sign saying, 'Please walk on the grass'. At first I thought it was a mistake, that they had in error left out the don't. But an American woman sitting on the seat with me assured me that it really wasn't an offence to walk on the grass. I have certainly never seen such a notice in England, where, if you are not absolutely forbidden to be carefree, you are not encouraged to tread on the carpet of green. I think one of the nicest sensations is to walk barefooted on grass, and if it is slightly damp with the dew, it is even better.

This American was one of the most amusing people that I met while abroad. She told me that her great-grandmother had come from England; that she herself was named Anne after the heroine of that name in *Persuasion*, because her grandmother doted on Jane Austen. Although her own mother heartily disliked the name Anne, the grandmother got her way because she was wealthy; though as she lived to be ninety-five the money was considerably decreased by then.

Anne told me she had had four husbands and divorced them all. 'I'm still friendly with them all, though, and they come to see me from time to time.'

'Not all at once surely? Otherwise it must be like a harem, or whatever the male equivalent is called. Are you looking for a fifth, or have you given up the whole idea of marriage?'

'I sure have not. Some place, somewhere, there must be the ideal man for me. God knows I know enough about love by now to satisfy all requirements. I sure just don't understand why it all goes sour; four times in all. I've had two Americans, a Canadian and a jack-of-all-trades. What are Englishmen like as husbands?' Here we went off into peals of laughter about the various deficiencies of the male sex.

Her grandmother and her mother had been married only once, so what was wrong with her that she was in and out of matrimony like a dog at a fair? She now had an analyst who, for extremely large sums of money, was sorting out her problems. Although she still didn't believe it, nevertheless it was a relief to be told that the fault was in her childhood; repressions and guilt had been growing all the time. Though, as she had the most loving parents, Anne couldn't see how the analyst arrived at these conclusions.

'But you know, Margaret,' she said, 'it's really a great comfort, and well worth the hard cash I have to pay out, to be told that all my marital troubles are because I'm unable to talk things out. My analyst believes that husbands and wives should be absolutely frank with each other, in more ways than one.'

Here she went off into giggles at the thought. For my part, I reckon that this idea of discussing everything can be a disaster. All this business of analysing love as though it is some mathematical problem that is bound to be solved if only you examine it from all angles seems to me to subject marriage to too great a strain.

I once had a neighbour who absolutely flourished on having these heart to heart talks with her husband. She loved dissecting his character and positively glowed with self-righteousness after one of these sessions, always telling me, 'Bob and I really got to know one another all over again.' Bob, poor fellow, was sick to death of all this 'knowing'; he heard it month after month. But he had his revenge, because there was one thing his wife didn't know, and that was that Bob had another lady friend who knew him only in the biblical sense of the word.

13 : Montreal

Although I looked forward with pleasure to seeing Albert and my family again, I still felt rather sad that my journey was nearly finished—a short stay in Montreal and then a plane back to England. I was to travel back on my own, but I wasn't worried, though I still intended to keep awake to be the first to give the alarm in an emergency—such as the rivets dropping out of the wings of the plane.

Our Toronto friends had told me that Montreal was very different from their own city or from Vancouver; that one needed to be a bit cautious in speaking to strangers or wandering off on one's own. It certainly was far less English than Toronto or Vancouver.

Actually, the only city that I had felt apprehensive of visiting was Chicago. I wanted to let people back home know that I had actually been in Chicago, but I also wanted to stay alive to tell them.

Our hotel in Montreal, the Ritz-Carlton, was the last word in quiet elegance and comfort. Even a face-lift hadn't destroyed the old-world character. Marble floors, huge leather armchairs, black and gold decorations and discreet lighting, all breathed of an old tradition, of a solid safe existence, yet nothing was shabby-genteel. Well, of course, it couldn't be, as a million dollars were spent on the hotel in 1964.

Although it exuded an air of long-forgotten charm and courtesy, there was nothing archaic about the service, which was quick and pleasant. As for the air-conditioning in my bedroom, it was really silent. And my bedroom was also elegant with gold and white wardrobe, carved chairs and a wash-basin set in marble.

A further attraction is supposed to be that Elizabeth Taylor and Richard Burton spent their wedding night there. Why this should be considered an attraction I don't know, unless it was as an exercise in the imagination.

One thing I was determined on: no more museums. I had seen enough, and more than I could appreciate. My escorts, whose duty surely it was to explain the exhibits, never did. They were interested only in what appealed to them, which seldom coincided with what I liked. Why they should have been surprised at this I don't know. It's all very well to say that art is universal, but time was when a painting mirrored an event, told a story or featured a recognizable face. What we now have are so-called painters and sculptors, who appear to see everything through a distorting mirror. No longer do we get traditional ideas of what constitutes art; what we do get are great splurging masses of irreconcilable colours, apparently daubed on to the canvas by a cross-eyed man wielding a white-wash brush. Or the canvas is adorned with 'bits' glued on—bus-tickets, match-boxes, old bills and bits of old bicycles, all the flotsam and jetsam of life. The same with sculpture. It really would be pleasant to view a head that resembled one. Instead we view contorted figures of which only the holes are worth looking at, or figures that are so elongated as to bear no relation whatever to the human anatomy.

What is even more amazing is that the producer of this junk gets his own exhibition. No wonder would-be artists seek to emulate this style. I went to one such show in London where I found six large green iron girders laid out cross-wise on the floor. What they were supposed to represent was a mystery to me; and the attendant couldn't elucidate. No doubt the layer of them could, but he was invisible, probably peering out and killing himself with laughter at the sight of adults walking round solemnly inspecting six iron girders.

Montreal is a fascinating blend of the old and new. All directions and street-names are written in French and English, with the French names always first.

Because Michael can speak and understand French—which I can't—he really came into his own in this city. So much so, that when we decided to do a walking tour of Old Montreal, he bought a guide-book written only in French, just to show how superior he was, I reckoned, but I wasn't impressed. I can do a lot of things he can't; though I seldom had the opportunity.

It took about two hours to walk around the old part, and very pleasant it was, too, though it would have been better still if I hadn't had to hang around such a long time waiting for Michael to translate the French into English. How much simpler to have bought a proper book!

Montreal was founded by two Frenchmen, who, in 1642, sent twenty-four French settlers to 'establish a settlement, to serve God, and to save the souls of the Indians'. Needless to say, the Indians were not consulted as to whether they wanted their souls saved by these interlopers. No doubt the Iroquois had their own god who had given them all this land; certainly if their souls were saved it was about the only thing that was, for with the advent of more and more white people, the Indians were pushed out.

Old Montreal is a maze of narrow streets, cobbled squares and tall, flat buildings with thick walls, pitched tin roofs and double chimneys. Most of the architecture is eighteenth century, and over five million dollars has been spent in restoring the Old Quarter—restoring, not ruining.

One of the cobbled squares reminded me of Paris with its flower stalls down the centre and smart little bistros lining the sides. We had a quick cold lunch in one of them and very good it was.

The church of Notre Dame is absolutely out of this world. It filled me with wonder that anybody could establish communication with God in such ornate surroundings; or indeed that all this splendour was needed if you already had a faith. It is built of limestone and the style is perpendicular Gothic. It was designed by two architects who were Protestants, but later became Roman Catholics; so the church had early converts. The ten bells were cast in Whitechapel Bell Foundry in London, and have pealed out for a hundred and twenty years. The first sight of the interior is so over-powering that one cannot take it in; in fact, several hours would be required to absorb all of it. One walks through colourful arches into a huge nave and then the full glory of the high altar is before one. In the light of flickering candles it glows like rose-red jewels, so rich in colour, with so much detail. There are three stained-glass rose windows in the ceiling, which is supported by slender fluted pillars. The ceiling is so high that it seems suspended in space. Millions of dollars must have been spent on, and perhaps still are poured into, the erection and up-keep of this building.

I eventually left feeling rather melancholy. Perhaps it was because I am an agnostic.

In the evening I had an interview with John Richmond of the *Montreal Star*. He quickly established himself in my affections by offering me a large gin and tonic as soon as Michael and I arrived at the Press Club in the Sherbourne Hotel. I was agreeably surprised at the comfort and spaciousness of the place; there were lots of armchairs and a long bar.

I had always thought that newspaper men lived a rushing, sweating life all day, while at night a collection of these hard-bitten men gathered in some sleazy pub to talk shop and use the spittoons to great advantage as they spat out their grievances about the world in general, and their editor in particular. That's how it always was portrayed in the old films about reporters. After leaving the pub these cynical men went back to a slummy bed-sitter and an embittered wife. Nothing was like that in the Press Club. Everybody looked prosperous and satisfied with life. If they privately knew that the world was coming to an end, the government about to fall or, even more important, Quebec ready to secede and become an independent state, they showed no indication of such knowledge.

I have only the vaguest memory of the kind of interview I gave, or indeed if I ever did one. But that was Michael's fault. He was there only to look after me, and this he signally failed to do by letting me drink several large gins. These were thoughtfully provided by John, who obviously understood that it's not possible to talk unless one's throat is well-lubricated. I do remember that an extremely large and jolly man was playing old music-hall songs on a piano, and that I stood beside him and belted out the words. Later on John and a friend had dinner with us, a very hilarious occasion. I was invited to have drinks with John on the following morning in a pub used by the reporters. I would have loved to do so, but Michael insisted that I had too much to do. The real reason was that, unbeknown to me, he had as usual booked a Gray Line Tour—for one only. Needless to say, that one was me. I sometimes felt as though I was living a life of perpetual motion on these never-ending coach tours. Somewhat nettled at missing John and the pub, I asked, 'Why me only? What about you?' For all I knew Michael could have been rushing out to the pub as soon as he had got rid of me. He couldn't accompany me, as, so he said, he had matters of world-import to settle which necessitated him and the telephone forming a partnership. As this was about the fifth time I had heard this story I didn't even bother to argue; I know when I'm beaten. I did occasionally wonder what my escorts thought they were there for. Both of them were so often immersed in their own affairs as to forget that they were supposed to be looking after me. It was a good job that I was capable of taking care of myself.

However, as it turned out, I had a most enjoyable two and a half hours owing to the attentions of a very interesting young American who sat next to me—well, not too young, about thirty-five. With that candour and friendliness that characterizes so many Americans, he introduced himself straight away as Stanley Aldridge from Idaho. He entertained me with the story of his life and adventures travelling all over the world as companion to an author who wrote books about far-flung places. 'Don't get the wrong idea,' he told me, 'I was with him to answer his correspondence, book planes and cars, and in general tend to his comfort. We had no personal relationship of an unhealthy nature.' I protested that such a thought would never enter my head, although in point of fact it was the very first thing that I had thought of. Why unhealthy? Is it unhealthy?

Stanley was a positive encyclopaedia of knowledge about Montreal, a city that he loved. He told me historical facts about the French being the first white people to arrive three hundred years ago. Although the British defeated the French in 1760, Quebec Province has still kept its French flavour and personality. In fact, Montreal is the second largest French-speaking city in the world, the largest being Paris. I couldn't even imagine Toby and Michael knowing anything of this, or if they did, being willing to impart all this interesting information to a complete stranger.

Stanley told me that a lot of the hostility between the French and the British is because the latter control most of the business and commercial interests, and that because half of the population is Roman Catholic, the priests are very powerful.

I told him that I would mention him in my book, so here it is. Thank you, Stanley Aldridge, for your entertaining company, and for listening to me also.

Our coach tour took in the McGill University—named after the founder—but I had no chance to talk to the students. We also had a splendid view of the islands where Expo '67 was held; it's certainly a splendid setting. Our driver told us that twenty million dollars were spent just on the entertainment, and that there were dolphins who answered commands given in French and English—I wonder if that's true.

I was horrified to hear that one of the sixty restaurants served stewed nightingale.

When I arrived back at our hotel, still full of energy, it was to find Michael exhausted by all the frustrations entailed in telephoning to other countries. At least, that's what he told me. However, when I told him that a visit to St Joseph's Oratory was a must, that every year over a million people visited it so why should we be left out, Michael agreed to come with me so long as we went in a taxi. Not for him the hardships of a bus or coach. One of his failings is that he has no idea of how to live a plebeian life. He was brought up in a society where cars and taxis are commonplace, and the idea that one can actually travel by train or bus is a novelty to him. Personally, I like trains and buses; there one can talk, and I like talking to people.

St Joseph's is built on a steep hill; to climb it on a cold and windy day was no easy task. According to the guide-book, thousands of people from all over the world assert that St Joseph has cured them when all the doctors failed. Certainly there is an impressive array of sticks and crutches left behind to prove this fact. It is a vast and almost indescribable place, with a 56-bell carillon, an organ of 5,811 pipes, a huge copper dome and a chapel lit by 10,000 candles.

I am sure that to thousands, even millions, of people, this church is a source of comfort and inspiration. But somehow I feel that if I wanted to pray, I would choose a simple unadorned place where nothing distracted the mind or eye from communion through prayer. This enormous elaborate edifice, with its attendant souvenir and art shops, its cafeteria and snack bars (even although the profits from these go to the upkeep of the church) seemed more a public monument than a place of prayer. I found it hard to reconcile the fact that already over ten million dollars had been spent to produce St Joseph's Oratory—and still it needs more money—with the Church's alleged concern with the poor and homeless. I felt depressed. This was not lightened by Michael, who, needless to say, had not wanted to come with me in the first place. He now insisted that, as this was a once-in-a-life-time visit, we should see everything in strict rotation. He refused to miss even the Stations of the Cross. These were spaced at intervals round the outside of the oratory, and climbing on this cold, wet and windy day did nothing to improve my spirits.

I was hoping to have a trip on the St Lawrence River, but all the seamen were on strike. Everywhere I went in America and Canada, somebody was on strike, just as they are in England. We drove across the Jacques Cartier Bridge but couldn't see the Seaway Lock in action because of the strike.

I was disappointed in the Indian Village of Caughnawaga but that was because I hadn't realized that it would be just the same as any other village. I didn't expect to see the Indians living in wigwams and sending out smoke-signals; but I suppose that I expected to find it different. In fact the Indians live in ordinary houses, work in the city, have cars and, according to our guide, make the best steeple-jacks in the world.

At least they don't put on a show for the tourists as the Hopi Indians did in the Grand Canyon. There they wore their coloured head-dresses, and performed war-dances and other tribal ceremonies. To me it seemed degrading that these once proud people had now, because of poverty, to caper about for the amusement of tourists.

There is a tiny church in Caughnawaga that is wholly Indian, plain, simple and just adorned with authentic Indian crafts.

Then came my last night in Montreal, my last night abroad. We had dinner in the garden room of the Ritz-Carlton, with dim coloured lights, soft melodious music, candles and flowers on the table, and good food and wine. A happy end to a wonderful journey! I thought of all that I had seen and done—regretted only that there was so much I had had no time to see.

Inevitably, I thought about my escorts, even, in my nostalgic mood, felt affectionate towards them for the, admittedly rare, occasions on which they had been kind and considerate. I suppose it was just possible that I could have had worse.

14: Looking Back

Now I am home again, I am constantly asked, 'What did you think of America? Did you like the people, the climate, the pace of life? Was it as violent as one reads in the papers? Is it true the Negroes are taking over?'

It's not so easy to give answers to all these questions. The country is so vast, the people so diverse; time is needed to form a judgment of any kind.

I would not want to live there in preference to living in England, neither did I consider that any city excelled the city I love, London; but I could easily live there if I had to do so.

That being said, there was so much that I liked and admired; from leisurely San Francisco, to Chicago, so alive and full of energy.

How can one compare America with England with its encompassable countryside, rivers, mountains and valleys? All is so vast in America. Landscapes seem to stretch to infinity; deserts are endless; rivers run for miles and miles; climate changes from state to state, as do the people. They are English-speaking, yet not English; with a political system based on ours but quite different; far more articulate in some ways than we are, more outspoken, far readier to converse with strangers.

More than a hundred years ago, Edward Dicey wrote, 'Never yet in history has a nation grown up under circumstances where all men have started equal, and where want and poverty have been practically unknown.' Well, they might have started equal, but they are not all equal now; neither are want and poverty un-

187

known. But I found an acceptance of this poverty and the so-called 'under-privileged'. I don't mean acceptance in the sense that nothing is being done about it; but acceptance of 'it isn't their fault that they are poor'.

In England, until very recently at any rate, it was almost a social crime to be poor and jobless—a legacy from Samuel Smiles perhaps. The general appearance of our officials, not all of them I'll admit, seemed to exude an aura of disapproval. It was your fault that you were poor and unemployed; you were shiftless.

From reading our newspapers one does occasionally get the impression that life in America, in the cities at any rate, is spent with half of the population looking over their shoulder in apprehension that the other half is about to knock them out. I saw no violence while I was there, neither did the public appear in mortal dread. They were shopping, walking, gossiping and working exactly the same as we do.

In spite of the enormous size of American newspapers, to me they seemed far less sensational than ours in the way the news was presented. Not only did you have to search through pages of advertisements before finding the news at all but also there were no great black screaming headlines of murder, rape and other sexual exploits.

I felt a sense of tremendous power about America. It appeared to be a country that could absorb anything and anybody without ever changing its character. Perhaps it is the immensity that does this; size alone does have an intimidating effect. Perhaps it is the people, so diverse in character and opinions.

I feel that a country that holds such a place of beauty, awe and silence as the Grand Canyon, and at the same time holds Las Vegas, is capable of everything. It is more than a country, it is a world, full of Americans who are not Americans but New Yorkers, Chicagans, Texans and New Englanders, 'our state above all'.

I think back to all the friendliness and hospitality I received; to the countless invitations, 'Do come and stay with us when you are over here again. Do write and let us know how you are.'

I think of some of those shrill American voices, but also of the warm and honeyed ones—mostly those of the men.

I remember the awful concoction that they have the nerve to

call tea, the so-called 'English muffins' that hadn't the faintest resemblance to them, the inevitable doughnuts. But, too, I remember the lovely food, the breakfast at Brennan's, dinner at Antoine's. The French, Japanese and Chinese cooking—superb, with one or two exceptions.

I remember, too, the 'American Hamburger', the unbeatable hamburger, always served in very clean cafés with polite and pleasant service.

I was surprised by the pleasant friendliness of so many shop-assistants, of the trouble they took to find my size, of the way they explained the American money and sales tax.

I have often been asked, 'Is it terribly expensive to live in America? How does New York compare with London for clothes, food and amusements?' Well, if you are living on American rates of pay, you can get by; but on English rates you haven't nearly enough. How our exchange teachers manage I don't know. It's a great temptation to spend and spend in New York; the shops are full of everything under the sun.

The different nationalities seem to settle in separate districts— German, Polish, Russian and Italian, the grandparents fiercely determined not to be assimilated into the American way of life, the children hovering uneasily between loyalty to their parents and their new country, the grandchildren frankly taking to the new life in every way.

Some Americans I met resented the least criticism of their way of life, telling me that unless one had lived in America for at least five years, one wasn't in a position to judge; it bore no relation to living to England. It did seem to me that the acquisition of wealth meant more to them than it does in England. But I suppose that the love of money is pretty much a human trait. We can't all get it, but that doesn't prevent anybody from trying. In America, in the absence of titles, great wealth proclaims the man.

Perhaps because America is a new country compared to ours, people at times denigrate it as being shallow and uncultured. This is absurd. Everywhere we went there were opera companies, symphony orchestras and theatres, and books by the thousand on every subject that one could imagine. It is certainly true in the entertainment sphere that good singers, bands and artists are there in abundance. As for the magnificent art galleries, museums and institutes, nowhere I'm sure could you see finer—and a great many are privately supported. Perhaps Americans are inclined to boast, but they have something to boast about. Even the man who told me that America saved us in both World Wars wasn't really far wrong.

I think that above all I liked the young people, the eighteen to twenty-five group. I like to believe that I understood their frustrations with an ever-increasing mechanized society, with its problems of race, government and what the future holds. Young people seem to become independent of their parents far sooner than they do in England. But they are not isolated and afraid, because they form their own groups within their age limits; they don't need adults to guide them.

I was talking to a very disgruntled father and mother of two teenage children in a café in San Francisco.

'They can't wait to leave home,' said the mother, and the father added, 'They think that they know all there is to know about life, morals, living and learning. They think that money buys everything—love, affection; they don't want us. Yet we looked after our parents all our life.'

How does one explain that it is such a different generation now living in a very different world, a world that perhaps the young believe will not last much longer?

Now I have finished, I think I loved America. I loved it for its sheer sense of adventure, the size and imagination of its cities; for the music of New Orleans, for the indescribable Grand Canyon, for its teeming life, its air of 'Here we are, like us or not.' Above all for all the kindness I met there.

Yes, indeed, I loved America.

50 23